Folk Customs at Traditional Chinese Festivities

Compiled by Qi Xing
Translated by Ren Jiazhen
Illustrations by Yang Guanghua

FOREIGN LANGUAGES PRESS   BEIJING

First edition   1988

ISBN   0-8351-1593-3
ISBN   7-119-00451-4

Published by Foreign Languages Press
24 Baiwanzhuang Road, Beijing, China

Printed by Foreign Languages Printing House
19 West Chegongzhuang Road, Beijing, China

Distributed by China International Book Trading Corporation
(Guoji Shudian), P.O. Box 399, Beijing, China

Printed in the People's Republic of China

CONTENTS

FOREWORD

Each and every one more or less has some childhood experience of looking forward eagerly to New Year celebrations. During the New Year holiday in China, "girls play with flowers while boys with firecrackers"; there are many tasty things to eat, colourful costumes to wear, and a most wonderful time can be had by all.

People in different places all have different ways to entertain themselves differently at festivities. For instance, they strike gongs, beat drums, perform lion dances and display dragon's lanterns during the Spring Festival; they row dragon boats at the Dragon Boat Festival on the fifth day of the fifth lunar month; they enjoy the moonlight at the Mid-Autumn Festival on the fifteenth day of the eighth month; and they climb up mountains on the Double Ninth Day on the ninth day of the ninth month. . . . The festive celebrations of the minority people include dialogue singing, dancing under moonlight, burning torches, splashing water on people, bull-fighting, snatching sheep or picking up the *hata* (ceremonial silk scarf) from horseback, horse-racing, wrestling, girl-chasing-boy games. . . . Indeed, a great variety of entertainment. These festivals, mostly having a source in one or more legends, mystify people and bring them hope and joy. So it is not the children alone who are eager to celebrate New Year or other festival occasions. Grownups, too, feel their hearts warm and gay in these days and find it difficult to suppress their hilarious excitement.

Since ancient times, the Chinese people have adopted over a hundred kinds of calendars. The most widely observed are the *Yang li* (the solar or Gregorian calendar) and the *Yin li* (the lunar or farming calendar). The former divides time into four seasons according to the rotation of the sun, a year into 12 months and 365 days, with every fourth year a leap year of 366 days and the second month of the year (February) 29 days. *Yang li* is now in use in various countries of the world, including China.

Yin li was designed in close connection with agricultural production, so it is also known as the farming calendar, which has been in use in this country since the Xia Dynasty about three to four thousand years ago.

Yin li is actually a mixture of the solar and lunar calendars with the length of time for one rotation of the moon counted as a month and having 12 months in a common year of 354 days, or 13 months in a leap year of 384 days. In ancient China, a year was divided into 24 solar terms (see Appendix 1), each of which has three climatic signs (*zheng hou*, 72 such signs altogether). These terms are directly related to farming and have been observed for the last several thousand years.

In China the various festivities in a year are usually calculated according to the lunar calendar developed over long years of history. These festivities and the customs observed on these occasions have strong national features and are part and parcel of the national culture we set great store by. In studying these customs, we will find that there is at least one or more anecdotes about practically every festival in China, anecdotes replete with the reminiscences of the nation's past, of its days of joy and misery. If we look back to the past, we can better understand our present; looking into the folk customs of the traditional festivities in China is like opening up a window of history for a peep into the sentiments and life of our forefathers.

Chinese festivities may be classified into the following four categories:

(1) Those commemorating an historical event or an historical figure. The Dragon Boat Festival on the fifth day of the fifth lunar month, for instance, is said to be a day in commemoration of the patriotic poet Qu Yuan; and the Clear and Bright Festival, a day to honour the memory of Jie Zitui, who was loyal to his sovereign.

(2) Those connected with a myth or a legend. The Spring Dragon Festival, for instance, is said to be the day on which the dragon raises its head; and the Double Seventh Night has a mythological and yet romantic background — the romance of the Cowherd and Weaving Maid.

(3) Those handed down year after year and developed from rites worshipping ancestors and deities. The La Ba Festival on the eighth day of the twelfth lunar month, for instance, is the day near the end of an old year and the beginning of a new one, on which secrifices are offered to heaven and earth, to all deities and to one's ancestry together, the word *la* itself having the meaning "together." Again, Jizao Jie is a survival of a rite offering sacrifices to the Kitchen God.

(4) Those taking place at the end of a year to say good-bye to the old or at the beginning of a year to greet the new, festivities on which people pray for good luck, such as New Year's Eve and the Spring Festival.

The minority peoples in China also have their unique festivities. There are festivities praying for a good harvest or celebrating one, such as the Onghor Festival of the Tibetans, the Duan Festival of the Shui people in Guizhou and the Torch Festival of the Yi people. There are festivities during which people buy and sell at a fair which also offers entertainment and amusements, such as the Mongolian people's Nadam Fair and the Third Month Fair of the Bai people. There are also festivities with a religious background, such as the Lesser Bairam of the Hui people and the Firecrackers Festival of the Dong people. There are very interesting anecdotes about these festivities. About the Water Splashing Festival of the Dai people, for instance, a legend has it that once there was a fiendish Devil Prince who feared almost nothing — water could not drown him, fire could not destroy him, neither a sword nor an arrow could kill him. He had seven wives in his harem, whom he took against their will. The seventh wife, a very clever woman, one day tactfully found out the secret of where he was vulnerable. In a night when he was asleep, she plucked a hair from his head, as he had said, and cut his head off with it. His head fell off and rolled down on the floor. But wherever it rolled, the place caught fire and when it rolled into a river, the river water began to boil and the fish in it died. And when it was buried, the whole place stank. So the seven women had to hold the head in their hands in turn, each for a day, and each time the take-over took place, the recipient of the head would be splashed with water. One day in heaven means a year on earth. Since then, every year on that day, people would splash water on each other. So the Water Splashing Festival is a day commemorating some heroines who had helped the people wipe out a devil.

The Torch Festival of the Yi people, for instance, is connected with a story about men's struggle against nature. It says that long, long ago, the forebears of the Yi people lived fairly well off in the Liangshan Mountains. The Heavenly King, envying them, sent a giant down to Liangshan to trample on the crops. When people protested and argued with the giant, he said arrogantly: "Well, I'll go back to heaven if any one of you succeeds in throwing me down." A young man named Bao Cong accepted the challenge and after a few rounds of wrestling, threw the giant down. The Heavenly King, upset, snatched up a handful of incense ashes and spread them over the fields down below, where they turned into pests starting to destroy the crops. So the Yi people lit torches to burn these pests to death.... While most of these stories are healthy and interesting, there are a few that are superstitious, and also some that describe unhealthy customs. With the popularization of science and progress in the ability to understand and transform nature, the unhealthy ones will eventually be eliminated.

If we liken a festival in our age-old national culture to a glistening pearl, and if we manage to put these pearls together to make them a beautiful pearl garland for our readers, it must be a very significant job indeed. With illustrations, this book gives, in a systematic way, the origins of the more important traditional festivities of the Han people and of the national minorities in China; it gives an account of their development and describes the very interesting customs observed at these festivities. We will be really happy if our readers find this book informative and useful in promoting a better understanding of China, China of yesterday and today.

Folk Customs at Han People's Important Festivities

1. Chun Jie (Spring Festival)

Origin of the "Nian"

The Spring Festival, the lunar New Year, is the most important traditional national festival in China.

Why is it the Spring Festival is also called *nian* or *xin nian* (New Year)? The Chinese character *nian* (年), philologically, is the earlier way of writing the character *ren* (稔), meaning harvest. In ancient lexicons, the character *nian* was placed under the department *he* (rice), because *nian* signifies a good harvest.

The term Spring Festival (*Chun Jie*) is a modern usage. For many thousand years, although China had had several reforms in its calendar system, the farming (lunar) calendar is the only one that has always remained in use. When people spoke of the New Year, they meant the lunar New Year. After the Revolution of 1911, which put to an end once and for all to monarchial rule in this country, the Gregorian calendar was officially adopted for use. To distinguish the *Xin Nian* (New Year) according to the Gregorian calendar from that according to the lunar calendar, people started calling the latter the Spring Festival, because it always falls sometime before or after Li Chun (Beginning of Spring).

1

There is some reason for people in ancient times to begin a year in a cold weather. This is because it is the time after "the autumn harvest and winter storage" and the time before "spring ploughing and summer weeding" — the slack season in farming, time for relaxation and celebrations after a year's toil, time for looking back to the past and looking forward to the days to come, time for a good, long rest before going to the fields to do beckbreaking work again.

"Amidst the Sound of Firecrackers...."

Wang Anshi of the Song Dynasty in his poem entitled "The First Day of the Year" gave a graphic description of the happy scenes of New Year celebrations in his time. His poem reads:

> Amidst the sound of firecrackers a year is out,
> With spring breeze instilling warmth into the "tu su"
>   wine.*
> As the morning sun shines over the gates of every household,
> The old Door God pictures are sure to be replaced by new
>   peachwood charms.

Setting off firecrackers and posting Door God pictures and couplets on the gates as described in the poem were the most popular customs observed in ancient China during New Year celebrations.

Setting off firecrackers is a practice handed down from the remote past — that of burning bamboo stems. Because bamboo stems have joints and are hollow inside, when they are burnt, the air inside after being heated expands so that the stem itself bursts open and cracks. Later on, people placed gunpowder

---

*A kind of herb wine people drank on New Year days, said to be a drink that expels the evil spirits.

into bamboo stems and invented *bao zhu* (exploding bamboo), or firecrackers. Still later, bamboo stems were replaced by paper rolls, and, by the close of the Qing Dynasty, there were already special workshops in China making all kinds of firecrackers.

At first, people set off firecrackers for the purpose of "keeping away evil spirits and exorcising ghosts, suppressing demons and seeking happiness." According to a legend there was a certain strange, nondescript beast whose body looked like a human being and who hid itself in remote mountains and was extremely savage. At the end of every year, it would come out to kill people and animals. However, it was afraid of light and noise. Whenever it heard the noise of firecrackers, it was so scared that it ran its head off. So, at the beginning and end of every year, the time the strange beast was supposed to make its appearance, people kept setting off firecrackers in order not to be disturbed by it.

In a book entitled *Dijing Suishi Jisheng* (*Wonderful New Year Days in the Imperial Capital*), the author gave a vivid description of how people in Beijing in the Qing Dynasty set off firecrackers on the first day of a year. "The noise of firecrackers," he wrote, "like roaring waves and thunderclaps, was heard in and outside the palace; it went on without letup for the whole night." Firecrackers, indeed, enlivened the New Year holiday, bringing great joy to people in general and children in particular.

During the Spring Festival, households hung peachwood charms on their main gates, or posted on them pictures of the Door Gods and couplets in bright red. This made places everywhere look splendidly festive.

Posting Door God pictures during the Spring Festival is a time-honoured custom. There are many interesting folktales about the Door Gods and it is difficult to say exactly who the Door Gods were. One of the sources says they were Qin Qiong

Door Gods.

and Yuchi Gong. It was said that when Li Shimin, or Emperor
Taizong of the Tang Dynasty, fell sick, he heard ghosts howling
in his dream. Next morning he told his dream to the court
officials. Qin Qiong and Yuchi Gong, both generals having
helped found the Tang empire, buckled on their armour, the
former holding a mace and the latter his iron staff, and stood
on guard in the night outside the door of the emperor's bed
chamber. Henceforth the emperor dreamed no more of ghosts.
To have peace in the night and yet feeling it was improper for
the two generals to stand guard night by night, the emperor told
a painter to draw the images of the two on a piece of paper and
hung it on the palace entrance as "Door Gods." When the

incident was made known, people of the common run eagerly did the same — posting pictures of Door Gods on their doors for the purpose of suppressing evil spirits.

New Year pictures are a folk art and posting them is a unique part of New Year celebrations. Themes of these pictures include "bumper harvest of the five principal cereals," bouncing fish (the word *yu* in Chinese means either fish or overflowing abundance), plump tots, flowers and birds. Historically famous for their New Year pictures are Yangliuqing in Tianjin, Weifang in Shandong Province, Taohuawu in Suzhou, Mianzhu in Sichuan Province, Wujiang in Hebei Province, and Foshan in Guangdong Province. Yangliuqing was once reputed to be the place where "every household knows how to apply colours on pictures and every family is good at drawing." Today, as many as over 100 million New Year pictures are produced a year in China.

Chun lian (spring couplets) are couplets posted on gates

New Year picture.

during the Spring Festival. They bear auspicious words such as:

The Best of Things and Treasures of Heaven;
Man of Outstanding Personality and Place of Good
*   Location.*

Days of Peace, Year In, Year Out;
Spring of Good Luck, This Year, Every Year.

Spring couplets originated from the "peachwood charms" in the ancient times. As early as the Spring and Autumn and the Warring States periods, there were already records saying that "Every household has peachwood charms hanging on the gates." They were tiny plates rectangular in shape and made of peachwood. In the New Year season, magic incantations were written on the plates which were nailed on the gates to "exorcise evil spirits and ask for blessings." They were also meant to send off the old and usher in the new. It was Lord Meng Chang of the State of Later Shu (934-965) in the period of the Five Dynasties and Ten States, who first wrote spring couplets on peachwood plates. This was told in the volume "The Shu Saga" in *History of the Song Dynasty*. It said that Lord Meng Chang "on every New Year Eve would ask his official in charge of

Spring couplets.

culture to compose a verse and write it on peachwood plates to be placed on the doors of his bed chamber." Once, the verse composed by the official failed to meet his approval, so he picked up a brush and personally wrote down the following couplets:

> *A New Year to Take in Surplus Fortune*
> *A Fine Festival to Call in Eternal Spring*

This was probably the first spring couplet ever written.

In the Song Dynasty, paper was used instead of wood plates for writing spring couplets. Then, the men of letters of the Imperial Academy often liked to write notes and hang them near the gates to the Imperial Palace. By the Ming Dynasty, encouraged by Emperor Taizu (Zhu Yuanzhang), spring couplets came into vogue. One New Year after he had made Nanjing his capital, Taizu issued an imperial decree requiring all officials, scholars and common people to post a pair of couplets on their gates. When he was travelling incognito and had seen these colourful spring couplets, he was pleased. Then he came to a house with nothing on its gates. He soon found out that the man who lived there was a man whose profession it was to castrate pigs and who was still looking for someone to write the couplets on his behalf. With a sense of humour, the emperor readily took out his own brush and wrote for him a pair of novel spring couplets:

> *Using both hands to chop and open up the road to life and death;*
> *Swing a knife to cut and sever the root of evil and trouble.*

This time-honoured practice is still being followed to this day except that with change of time, things said in these couplets are quite different from those of the past. They now either describe the flourishing national construction or sing the praise of the wonderful sights of the land, or give expression .to people's wishes for a still better future....

7

New Year Delicacies

The Chinese people, traditionally, are industrious and thrifty, leading a somewhat simple life. But they eat a lot of good food during the Spring Festival. The book *Wonderful New Year Days in the Imperial Capital* listed all kinds of foods Beijing inhabitants in the Qing Dynasty ate during the Chinese New Year. "Speaking of food to entertain guests," it observed, "there are carved fruits at tea and assorted chafing dishes at dinner. For hot refreshments, there are rolls deep-fried in goose fat, steamed buns stuffed with minced pork, sticky rice cake, light brown broomcorn millet cake; for main dishes served with wine, there is salted chicken, cured pork, goose meat pickled in wine, dried fish, pheasant meat, dried venison and breast meat of rabbit; there are all kinds of fruit and nuts to eat, such as pine nuts and hazel nuts, lotus seeds, walnuts, peaches, apricots and melon seeds, chestnuts, dates and dried longan pulp, haw jelly, grapes, white pomegranate seeds, pears, apples, oranges, tangerines and red bay berries. There is also sea food and game, and home-made dishes as well as refreshments bought at food shops."

Rare game and seafood in the list were, of course, quite beyond the means of the ordinary homes, but such a long list certainly had not included all the food of a greater variety eaten at the Spring Festival. In north China, the most popular food enjoyed by the rich and the poor alike was *jiao zi*, or dumplings. It is eaten on the thirtieth of the twelfth lunar month and the following day, the First Day of the First Month. *Jiao zi* was known in the old days as *bian shi*, meaning flat food. *Qing Bai Lei Chao* (*Collected Random Notes by People in the Qing Dynasty*) has an item which says: "*Jiao*, a kind of refreshment made either of wheat or rice flour with stuffing inside . . . , the steamed ones are called *tangmian jiao* (hot flour dumpling) while those boiled in water are called *shui jiao*, or water dumpling." People in this country have considered them their favourite dish since antiquity. This is probably because it is a combination of both staple (flour) and non-staple food (meat and vegetable inside), easy to prepare and good. Made like a *yuan bao* (a shoe-shaped gold or silver ingot used as money in ancient China), it is supposed to augur good fortune. A dumpling may be stuffed with sugar (suggesting a life so sweet), with coin (suggesting a lot of money to spend throughout the year), with peanuts (known as the longevity nut in Chinese, suggesting long life) or with dates (both dates and the word "early" in Chinese are pronounced as *zao*) and chestnuts (*li zi* meaning either chestnut or having a son) (a combination of *zao* and *li zi* suggesting begetting a son very soon).

In south China, during the New Year, rice for meals is washed clean several days beforehand — called *wan nian liang* (grain for ten thousand years) to suggest that every year there will be food grain to spare. Dishes on the dinner table naturally included chicken, duck, fish and meat. Pastries consumed in the south during the New Year are more varied than those in the north. *Nian gao* (New Year cake) is a must, the more sticky the better, because the words "sticky cake" are pronounced the same as *nian gao* and so *sticky New Year cake* can be interpreted as "soaring high every year." In Guangzhou and its vicinity, people in New Year offer their visitors a box of cakes of all kinds, and eat steamed pastries, triangular fried dough, steamed cake, turnip cake, nine-layer cake.... In Huaian, Jiangsu Province, people have lotus seed soup, date soup, both sweetened, melon seeds, dates, and cakes before meals; they keep chanting *tian tian mi mi* (life sweet like honey) when eating sugar, and *bu bu deng gao* (promotion step by step) when eating cakes (*gao*, or cake, also means high and mighty), or *zao sheng gui zi* (have a brilliant son early) when eating dates (*zao zi* in Chinese). In Shaoxing, Zhejiang Province, people drink tea on New Year's Day with olive and kumquat in it. For breakfast on the day, ball dumplings are served to signify reunion. The aged eat vegetables instead of meat or fish that day.

New Year Celebrations

On the eve of the Spring Festival, it is a folk custom to stay up late or all night and pray for peace in the coming year. That night every house is brightly lit in the hope that anything that may bring people bad luck hidden in every nook and corner will be forced to disappear under the dazzling light. In some places, people light torches made of pine tree branches, reeds or bamboo at first light to illuminate the house both inside and out — a practice known as *ting liao*, meaning a fire in the courtyard.

New Year is ushered in at midnight, 12 sharp. In the old days, on *yuan dan* (meaning the first morning), the first thing to do was set off firecrackers and burn incense, welcome deities back (who are supposed to have left for heaven at the end of the previous year) and pay respects and offer sacrifices to forbears. On that day, everybody, men and women, old and young, put on new clothes and visited relatives and friends to exchange greetings by making a bow with hands folded in front, kowtowing and saying nice things such as *gong xi*! (congratulations), wishing one the best of everything during the New Year, or "greater happiness and long life," or "wishing you happiness vast as the Eastern Sea and a life everlasting as the Southern Mountain." When the younger generation extend their New Year greetings to their seniors, the latter will give them money wrapped in red paper, called *ya sui qian* (money to keep for the year). The children, wearing new clothes, new shoes and new hats, with *ya sui qian* in their pockets, are free to buy whatever they fancy — fruit, sweets or firecrackers — and enjoy themselves to their hearts' content without all those don'ts they usually have to bear in mind. On that day,

10

grownups do nothing but sit idly by and chat, no unpleasant subjects, of course.

On the second day, after breakfast, there are exchanges of visits between friends and relatives who will bring each other New Year cakes, oranges and tangerines and crunchy candy as gifts. The host will offer his guests first tea and then cigarettes and after some brief preliminaries the guests will ask to leave to call on other friends or relatives. Some people go to the temple of their clan, where food and wine are served, playing games and "shooting the breeze." This is known as *tuan nian*, meaning members of the clan getting together for a reunion and celebrating the New Year together.

The third day is known as the "day to send off poverty." That day, there will be no mutual visits between friends and relatives. People just stay home and sweep clean their houses; all rubbish, waste paper and the like are taken to an open field and destroyed in fire. At this juncture, they must burn incense and candles, set off firecrackers, kowtow and bow with hands clapsed as a way to clear away filthy things and send off poverty to let in wealth and happiness.

The fourth day is the day for women to go and see their own parents. Putting on new dresses, bringing gifts and their children along, they leave in threes or fives, talking to each other on their way along the narrow path in the countryside. It must be the happiest day in the year as far as they are concerned.

The fifth day is said to be the day all deities in heaven will come down to the mundane world for an inspection tour. Before the idols are laid "the three secrifices" (slaughtered ox, sheep and pig, or chicken, fish and pig), with fruit. People bend in worship, asking the idols for blessings.

All in all, every day from the New Year Eve to the fifteenth day of the first month, which is the Lantern Festival, there are some kinds of activities every day. In the old days, most of the

11

New Year activities were prompted by superstitious beliefs and there was much gambling. As people become more and more civilized, they are giving up these corrupt customs of their own volition.

Gong and Drum Contest and Lion Dance

Lion dances and drum and gong contests are grand events in the New Year celebrations, especially in the countryside in the south. The sound of drums and gongs continues here and there all day long during the season up to the fifteenth day of the first month. The contest is a part of mass recreational activities with every village sending a team consisting of a drum, a pair of cymbals and several gongs. The drummer acts as the conductor and the other players perform to the rhythmic beats of the drum. When the playing comes to a climax, all teams strike their instruments with a vengeance, each trying to overpower others in the noise they make. Thus, there is a deafening sound like a seismic sea wave, or like thousands of horses galloping at the same time, which creates a most lively atmosphere in the otherwise quiet countryside.

Lion dancing is a traditional folk sports activity. From the fourth day of the New Year to the fifteenth of the first month, there are lion dance groups, each composed of seven to more than ten people, touring from village to village. All performers wear the same kind of coats, trousers, shoes and headgear, with a sash round their waist, armed with swords and clubs to give people an impression of grandeur. The lion's head is made of paper in a traditional shape: cat's head, rooster or the bull-fighting lion. The lion's head is complete with painted eyes, nose, mouth and tongue, decorated with bells tinkling on tassels. The body is a motley piece of cloth. The dance is performed by one fellow holding the lion's head with both hands and another bowing low and hunching his back at the

Lion Dance at the Spring Festival.

lion's tail. They will ape the various gestures of a lion to the accompaniment of drums and gongs. Two fellows disguise themselves as monkeys and another two as clowns, dancing and somersaulting, while making funny gestures to amuse the public. Lion dancing has a long history in this country and its performers are all very skillful dancers, some excelling in the head's movements, some in somersaulting and rocking on the ground, some acting boldly but nimbly to perform stunts, some moving in an exquisite but humorous way. Among the commonly seen performances are the lion playing with a ball, the "gladiator" teasing the lion, the lions at play and the lion and its cubs.

There are many other good recreational activities during the Spring Festival, such as walking on stilts, dragon lantern show, rowing land boats and riding bamboo horses. In many places there are stage shows with such traditional repertoire as *Monkey Subdues the White-Bone Demon*, adapted from the classic novel *Journey to the West,* and *A Tale of the White Snake* based on a popular folk story.

Changdian Fair in Beijing

Fairs are a time-honoured custom in China, instrumental in forging economic links between town and countryside and promoting trade. The local fairs, with strong national features, create a festive mood. There are fairs all over China during the Spring Festival. Here we introduce two unique ones, one in the north and the other in the south — Beijing's Changdian Fair and the Flower Market in Guangzhou.

Back in the Qing Dynasty, Changdian in Beijing was already one of the nationally famous fairs in the country. From the first to the fifteenth day of the first month, stalls lined streets several kilometres long with Liulichang as the centre of activities. There were roadside opera and acrobatic shows at the fair. For sale at the fair were all kinds of merchandise, ranging from books, paintings and curios to sundry goods for daily use, toys, light refreshments with a local flavour and fruit in season. Men of letters or people of means may look for precious stones and bronze seals, engraved inscriptions, rubbings, jewelry and curios; others could always find the things for daily use they wanted. As to children, the fair was virtually a **paradise** where they could have sugar-coated haws on a stick, or buy a very magnificent kite or pinwheel for a song. At the fair, people moved shoulder to shoulder in an endless stream, the aged helped by their kinsmen and the young led by their parents. "A Visit to Changdian," written in the Qing Dynasty, gave a graphic account of the busy scenes at that time: "The place was empty at other times with rarely any human souls in sight. But in the first lunar month of a year, men and women in the whole city came to visit this place, some by cart, others coming hand in hand in a constant flow." Lu Xun, a great man of letters of contemporary China, came to Changdian at every Spring Festival when he was living in Beijing. In one year, he visited the place altogether seven times within a fortnight (as told in his own diary).

Guangzhou's Flower Market

The flower market in Guangzhou is another Spring Festival fair with a widespread fame. According to the old tradition, it takes place for three days and nights before the first day of the first month, closing at two-thirty in the early morning of the New Year's Day.

Situated south of the Five Ridges, Guangzhou has a mild climate and flowers in all seasons. During the Spring Festival, flowers grown in the nine counties on both banks of the Pearl River as well as in the Guangzhou suburbs, keep pouring into the city like a tidal wave. Practically all the main and back

14

streets in Guangzhou are drowned in a sea of flowers. People often use the expression "a flowery street five kilometres long" to describe the grandeur of the fair.

At the fair people have all kinds of flowers to choose from, including bright-coloured peach blossoms, elegant and unsullied chrysanthemums, graceful narcissus and kumquats, which are symbolic of good luck. . . . In a sea of flowers, one may take a look at the famous palace lanterns from Foshan and listen to the light Cantonese (Guangdong) music — a sumptuous artistic feast not to be forgotten.

Spring Festival in Imperial Palaces

The emperors of the Ming and Qing dynasties attached major importance to the Spring Festival and observed more elaborate rituals than the common people.

A Ming emperor would receive congratulations from his court officials on the first day of the first month. The day before, an imperial throne would be placed in the Feng Tian (Rule by the Will of Heaven) Hall. At daybreak, in its courtyard, imperial guards of honour lined the road used by the emperor. Outside the Feng Tian Gate flew myriads of pennants. At both sides of the compound, from the stone steps that led to the hall to Wu Men (the main entrance to the palace), palace guards stood on duty. At the first beating of the drum on the Wu Men Gatetower, ranking court officials and military officers in official dress assembled outside the gate. At the second beating of the drum they entered the palace through the side gates in two files and stopped at the east and west sides of the steps, standing there facing north. At the third beating of the drum, the emperor, wearing the royal ceremonial robe and the crown, seated himself on the throne to receive greetings from his officials and generals. One representative of the officials would read aloud a congratulatory message singing the

Ming court acrobats
at the Spring Festival.

praise of the emperor. The message may have read as follows: "Your humble servant so and so, on this New Year's Day, finds everything on earth having a new start. We hereby respectfully wish Your Majesty the emperor good health. May Your Majesty be blessed and rule according to the will of heaven with eternal prosperity." In reply the emperor would say, "Let's celebrate this New Year's Day together." The Master of Ceremonies would then cry: "Raise the tablet" (meaning hold high the ceremonial ivory tablet with both hands), "Bow" and "Salute." At this juncture all officials and officers would make an obeisance by cupping one hand in the other at the chest and shouting three times *wan sui* (live ten thousand years long). All officers and men present also would shout in unison *wan sui* three times. By then, the band would strike up music and firecrackers would be set off; after the emperor had retired to the inner palace, all court officials would also withdraw one by one. This ended the New Year celebration ritual. Sometimes the ceremony would be followed by a grand banquet.

In the Qing Dynasty, the emperor gave a dinner reception at Baohedian (Hall of Preserving Harmony) on the New Year Eve, attended mainly by leaders of the minority peoples, envoys from the satellite states and ranking officials of the first and second grades. The Imperial Household Administration set ninety tables in both sides of the hall with wine and dishes of food. The floor beside the tables were paved with coir mats and the mats were again covered with felt rugs. Each table served two, who sat on the rug cross-legged. The two dinner tables in front of the emperor's throne were elevated.

Those who attended the banquet took their places as arranged beforehand. After the emperor had seated himself on the throne, all present prostrated on the spot and kowtowed to him before they too could sit down on the rug on the floor. The emperor was the first to sip some wine, followed by the rest. During the banquet the royal band played the musical movement All Was Quiet and Peaceful on Earth. When music came to a stop, there were performances of Mongolian reed instruments, songs of the Tibetan and Hui regions and the happiness dance. This dance was performed by a dozen or so peers and palace guards, pair by pair, with a group of guards as accompanists singing Manchurian songs and another group making rhythmic sounds by scraping wicker dustbins with chopsticks. It was then followed by more performances outside the hall. The first on the programme was the *qing long* dance, performed by cavalrymen of the Eight Banners (Manchurian military-administrative units). Wearing armour and masks, carrying bows and arrows, with banners in the colour of their own unit on the back, and riding horses or walking on stilts, they performed the dance of fighting bears and tigers (men in disguise). There were also the Korean clown's dance (mostly somersaulting), the miscellaneous show (acrobatics) of the Hui region and Jinchuan. Finally, there was the lion dance. At this moment, the emperor would get to his feet and all officials would all stand up after kowtowing to him. They were then free to bring home the food on their own table. After the emperor had left, the attendants too were allowed to take away the remaining pastries and fruit on the tables, known as "snatching and seizing the banquet delicacies," which brought an end to the royal banquet.

2. Yuanxiao Jie (Lantern Festival)

Its Origin

The fifteenth day of the first lunar month is an important traditional festival in China. Books written in ancient times refer to it as *shang yuan* (upper part of the year) *jie* (festival) and the night as *yuan ye* (night with the first full moon) or *yuan xiao* (evening), the last term being in use to this day. Members of a family will get together to mark the occasion. Because there is an exhibition of lanterns that night, *Yuanxiao Jie* is also known as the Lantern Festival.

This festival can be dated back to the Warring States Period, when people observed the custom of watching lanterns under moonlight in that night. At first, it was the day for offering sacrifices to the Sun God, then known as the "world's very first emperor of the East" or "the Lord of the East." People began to mark the Lantern Festival in the Han Dynasty. In ancient Chinese history, after the death of Liu Ying (the Han emperor Hui), his consort Queen Lu for a while usurped the power of the state. After she died, Zhou Bo, Chen Ping and others who were intent on keeping the Liu's Han Dynasty going, jointly started a campaign to get rid of the Lus and made Liu Heng the emperor, later known as Emperor Wen. The new emperor, who, by pooling the good ideas of his court officials, governed

Lantern Festival.

his country in a conscientious way, while giving relief to the needy, with the result that the Han empire was revived to become powerful and prosperous again. Because the Lus were got rid of on the fifteenth day of the first month, the emperor would leave his palace in civilian dress that night every year to celebrate the anniversary day with the men on the streets. In ancient times, the word *ye* (night) and *xiao* (evening) were synonyms and the first month of a year was called the *yuan* (primary) month, so Emperor Wen named the fifteenth day of the first month the Yuanxiao Jie.

Lantern Exhibition

This is a custom that has prevailed from antiquity to this day, something the people of China cherish. According to the Song Dynasty book *Dongjing Menghua Lu* (Memoirs of the Eastern Capital), "On the night of the fifteenth of the first month, tall awnings were pitched up in front of the imperial palace. People gathered at both sides of the road used by the emperor, where performing arts of all kinds were staged side by side by different theatrical troupes. The sound of music and the din of human voices could be heard more than ten li* away."

This custom at first had something to do with the night curfew in ancient China. Since the Zhou Dynasty, common people had been forbidden to go outdoors or get together in the night. Such a rigid convention was, of course, not becoming to the festive mood in the first month of a year, for it suppressed the need of the people to enjoy themselves. The rulers, who wanted to have fun themselves, and, more important, to pacify the people under their rule and make the capital appear peaceful and prosperous, thus relaxed the night curfew during the festival. Accoding to the volume "On Recreation" in the

---

* 1 *li* = 1/2 km.

Han Dynasty's *Shi Ji* (*Records of the Historian*), the rite of sacrifice to the heavenly king took place throughout the night until the dawn. This was perhaps the occasion that night curfew was lifted for the first time. Later, it provided people with a chance to go out in the night and watch the lanterns. Displaying lanterns on that night was a common practice by the Southern and Northern Dynasties. Emperor Jian Wen of the Liang Dynasty in a prose article on lamps described the lanterns at the Lantern Festival. He listed a number of them: oil lanterns and lacquer lanterns, some burning incense, some burning candles. The lights of the moon and the lanterns beamed together, forming reflections in the water. People enjoyed watching these lanterns and also the shows staged that night.

In the Tang Dynasty, the Lantern Festival was a three-day national holiday and all government offices were closed on the fourteenth, fifteenth and sixteenth. Curfew was lifted for three

A Ming wood carving of the Lantern Festival.

nights for city residents to go out and have as much fun as they liked; even if they came near the palace wall the palace guards were told not to interfere. In the second year of Xian Tian (A.D. 713) under the reign of the Tang emperor Xuan Zong the palace gates were kept wide open on the night of the festival and outside the gates, there was "a lantern wheel two hundred feet in height . . . on it were fifty thousand lanterns which made the wheel look like a tree in blossom." Over a thousand palace maids and another thousand young girls and women in the city of Changan were gathered "to sing under the lantern wheel for three days and nights." (See *Chao Ye Jin Zai*, or *Notes on Court and Civilian Affairs*, written in the Tang Dynasty.) Since then, emperors of the succeeding dynasties would watch lanterns from an imperial tower on the night of the festival to show that they were ready to share the fun with their subjects. The royal household, the Taoist and Buddhist temples as well as the households of the nobility and the rich would all erect tall awnings and towers decorated with colourful fabrics and vie with each other in making lanterns with unusual designs at a fabulous cost. So both the main thoroughfares and back lanes were flooded with lanterns which made the night as bright as day.

In the Song Dynasty, the lantern exhibition was prolonged from three nights to five and was held on a still greater scale. There were lanterns made of coloured glass, or even of white jade, in various odd shapes. Drawn on these lanterns were landscapes, human figures, flowers and birds. The more eye-catching ones were those made in the shape of dragon boats, those piled up to form a turtle-like hill, and those that formed pavilions, terraces and towers. There were also lantern pagodas, lantern hills, lantern balls and lantern arches. People would span the busy streets with coloured ropes on which lanterns hung — this was called lanterns across the street. To encourage people to come and watch lanterns displayed along the road used by the emperor, the court made it a rule to give a cup of wine to any one who came. The colourful scenes of the lantern exhibition at the festival were vividly presented in a lyrical poem by the Song Dynasty poet Xin Qiji. It reads:

> An easterly breeze prompts a thousand trees to bloom in a night,
> It also blows them off, which fall like a rain of stars.
> Carved cabs drawn by steeds leave the whole street a pleasant smell.
> The flute is heard in the air,
> The light of the jade-like lanterns are glittering.
> All night the lanterns of fish and dragon keep dancing. . . .

By the Ming Dynasty under Zhu Yuanzhang, the lantern exhibition was again prolonged to as long as ten nights. In the Ming and Qing dynasties theatrical performances were staged alongside the exhibition.

In recent years, with the improvement of the people's material and cultural life, lantern exhibitions in various parts of the country became all the more colourful, unprecedented in scale. Lanterns lit at the festival are such a wonderful sight: Overhead is the bright moon and down below are myriads of lanterns. The beams in the sky and the beams on earth meet to brighten each other. Other amusements at the festival include playing on a swing, flourishing dragon lanterns, staging plays, displaying fireworks, walking on stilts, and performing the boat dance (a sham boat made of bamboo without a bottom, tied on the waist of woman dancer making movements as if she is rowing a boat).

Lantern-making soon became a distinct craft, thanks to the development of lantern exhibitions at the Lantern Festival. There is no record of when the making of fancy lanterns began. It was said that the master carpenter Lu Ban of the Warring States Period started making palace lanterns to decorate the palatial edifices he was building. Thus it may be said that the Chinese people have been making fancy lanterns for at least over two thousand years. Fancy lanterns have multifarious shapes and multifarious designs. Among the human figure lanterns are "Chang E Flying to the Moon,"* "Xi Shi Plucking Lotus Seeds"** and "Liu Hai Teasing His Toad."*** The flower and fruit lanterns include water lily, grape, melon, lotus root, peony, persimmon and tangerine. The animal lanterns consist of those of deer, crane, dragon, horse, monkey, phoenix, goldfish, carp, frog and shrimp. Today fancy lanterns at the Lantern Festival are even more varied, each vying with the other in originality and beauty. They include also such traditional ones as the revolving lanterns with paper-cut figures inside, the lotus lantern and the peacock lantern. The revolving lantern is so called because there are paper-cut generals on horseback, which keep revolving. At the bottom of the lantern there is a wheel and when a candle under the wheel is lit, the hot air creates a convection which keeps the wheel moving so that the paper figures also keep moving, one chasing after the other.

Now there are electric wall lamps depicting an episode ("Monkey Subdues the White-Bone Demon") in the classic novel *Journey to the West*; and electric-powered lanterns showing a peacock erecting its tail coverts and spreading its fan, "the heavenly maid spreading flowers," or "a goldfish blowing bubbles."

---

*Chang Ê is said to be the wife of an ancient tribal chief and archer. She steals the elixir from her husband, who has got it from a goddess, and administers it herself with the result that she becomes an immortal and flies to the moon.
**Xi Shi is said to be a beauty, sent by the King of Yue as a tribute to the King of Wu of a neighbouring state, who had vanquished her own.
***Liu Hai is a fairy boy in ancient mythology. He wears a lock of hair on his forehead, has a string of cash in his hand and rides on a golden toad. — *Tr.*

In northeast China, people like to make all sorts of lanterns with ice, which are exquisitely wrought to resemble things in real life. The frame of a fancy lantern may be made with materials like bamboo, iron, wood, wicker, wheat stalks and animal horns, covered with coloured paper, silk, gauze, polyester fibre, glass or plastic cloth.

In the night of Yuan Xiao, there are lantern riddles at lantern exhibitions. Riddle is a game that originated in the Spring and Autumn Period. It was a time when many wise rulers emerged, many states scrambled for power and many professional strategists approached sovereigns to sell their ideas on how to gain an upper hand in the game of power politics. These people often did not say directly what was on their minds but used hints, which in a way were riddles in their embryonic form. Statements with certain implications were known at that time as *sou ci*, or *yin yu* (hidden statements). They developed into riddles in the days of the Three Kingdoms. Thus, riddles that touch on almost anything under the sun, mystifying and misleading, are now written on lanterns of different shapes for people to try to solve. Those who get the answer often win a prize.

Something Nice to Eat

It is the tradition for every household to eat *yuan xiao* (here it means a ball-like glutinous rice flour dough stuffed with sweet things) that day, symbolic of family reunion, affection and happiness in China. It is also known as *fu tuan zi* (floating ball) or *tang yuan* (balls in soup).

Folklore tells why people started eating *yuan xiao* at the Lantern Festival. It happened in the days of Emperor Wu of the Han Dynasty. One snowy day, Dongfang Shuo, a man of letters and one of the emperor's courtiers, went to the royal garden to pluck some plum blossoms for His Majesty. There he saw a maid-in-waiting named Yuan Xiao about to jump into a well and die. He rescued her. It turned out that the maid had missed her dear ones so much at festive occasions and was so desperate that she wanted to live no more. Dongfang, in great sympathy with her, thought out a way for her to see her family. He told her to wear a red dress and go to the main street of the capital to read out a statement in the name of the Jade Emperor in Heaven: "I, the God of Fire, am here by order of the Jade Emperor to burn down Changan City. His Celestial Majesty will watch me performing my duty from the Southern Heavenly Gate up there." Those who heard her took her seriously and hastily asked for mercy. So the girl in red replied: "Well, if you really want to avert this disaster, take this note to your emperor and let him think of a way out." So saying, she passed them a note written on a piece of red paper and left.

The note was sent to the emperor, who opened it to find the following message: "Changan is doomed. The emperor's palace will be burnt down in a celestial fire on the sixteenth with red flames glowing in the night."

Emperor Wu was stunned and asked Dongfang Shuo for advice. Dongfang said with presence of mind: "I understand that the God of Fire is fond of *tang yuan* and that the maid Yuan Xiao is very good at making them. The God of Fire may also know that the *tang yuan* she makes is tasty. I would suggest that she make *tang yuan* in the evening of the fifteenth and Your Majesty burn incense and offer it to the God of Fire as a sacrifice. Your Majesty will also issue a decree ordering each and every family in the capital to make *tang yuan* for the God of Fire, who might be pleased and change his mind. Your Majesty will then tell people in the capital, officials and civilians alike, to make lanterns and hang them on the main streets and back lanes, in courtyards and on doors and display fireworks as if the whole city is ablaze on the night of the sixteenth. The Jade Emperor watching from the Southern Heavenly Gate might very well be hoodwinked and mistake this as the city on fire."

So Emperor Wu did as Dongfang proposed. On the sixteenth of the first month, after sunset, the whole city was brightened by lanterns and fireworks everywhere. Yuan Xiao's young sister too came with her parents to watch the scene. When she caught the sight of a huge palace lantern with the name of Yuan Xiao on it, she cried out in hilarious excitement: "My sister, there is my sister Yuan Xiao!" When Yuan Xiao heard this she rushed to her parents and the whole family was reunited to tell each other how they had missed each other. Since then people have taken Yuan Xiao Festival as an opportunity for a family reunion. And because the *tang yuan* for sacrifice made by the palace maid Yuan Xiao was the best, people now prefer to call it *yuan xiao*.

Although *yuan xiao* made in different places have different flavours with different tastes, they all are symbolic of family reunion and are liked by everybody. The Song Dynasty poet Jiang Baishi had verses like these:

> *The man of high position draws up the curtain*
> *To look at the road used by the emperor.*
> *There the treasured thing on the market*
> *Is now available.*

Here the poet referred to *yuan xiao* as a treasured thing, which means that it must be rather costly at that time. Today, *yuan xiao* in China has many different flavours — sugar, cassia, haw, date paste, the "five ingredients," black sesame, plum, bean paste, or even cocoa. Besides, they can be bought at a moderate price. Boiling and eating *yuan xiao* at the Yuan Xiao Festival is a traditional joy.

3. Chunlong Jie (Spring Dragon Day)

Dragon in Legends

"The dragon raises its head on the second day of the second month." That is what is said in a legend and the day is called Spring Dragon Day. The third of the twenty-four solar terms on the lunar calendar (see Appendix 1), Jing Zhe, falls on or near that day. It is said that dragons which have wakened up after hibernation begin to growl and shake their tails on that day, causing thunderclaps.

But what is a dragon like? Nobody has ever seen one. According to archaeologists after years of research, there never has been such a thing as a dragon. But in mythology the dragon is an animal with the body of a snake, antlers of a deer, talons of an eagle and the face of a horse! Its body has scales that glitter like gold and its beards are like two ribbon bands. The dragon image was established at the dawn of civilization in a primitive society. At that time, every clan or tribe had a totem of its own, that is, the picture of an animal — an ox, a horse, a tiger, a deer or a snake. The clan which ruled the Xia Dynasty had the snake as its totem and another clan which ruled the Shang Dynasty made the bird its totem. . . . Due to the incessant conflicts and annexations taking place between the clan communes, the totem as a symbol of a particular clan, too, changed constantly. Thus, the snake clan, having annexed the eagle clan, might revise its totem by adding a pair of talons on the body of the snake. Later it also annexed the deer clan, so two antlers were added to its totem as a result. . . . As time went by, an odd-looking "dragon" came into being.

The image of the dragon, too, has undergone changes in the last several thousand years. According to a legend, dragons can be divided into *tian long* (dragon in heaven) which rides the clouds and flies in a misty sky, and *pan long* (curled dragon), which cloisters itself somewhere on earth. The earliest record about *tian long* is found in *Feng Shan Shu* (*Book on Offering Sacrifices to Heaven and Earth*): About four thousand years ago, Huang Di (the Yellow Emperor, supposed to be forebear of the Chinese nation) had a huge iron tripod cast at the foot of Jingshan Mountain in present-day Henan Province. Upon the completion of the tripod he mounted a dragon and ascended the sky. As early as the Tang and Song dynasties, Dragon King Temples were built to ask the Dragon King to give people his blessings and promise a good climate for farming (for dragons are supposed to be in charge of rainfall, lakes, rivers and seas). This custom of asking the favour of the Dragon King has been handed down from generation to generation. *Pan long* was identified with Yu the Great, whose accomplishments in harnessing rivers had won popular support and acclaim. He was looked on as the scion of the dragon family. Since then, the dragon has become the symbol of the sovereign in China. Emperors of every dynasty without exception claimed themselves to be the "real dragon" or the "son of heaven." Thus, in the Qing Dynasty, the Chinese national flag actually had a dragon embroidered on it; the dragon then stood for supreme authority.

Customs at the Festival

Customs observed at the festival vary from place to place. In Shaanxi, women did not do needlework on that day for fear, it is said, that their needles might pierce a dragon's eye, causing retaliation. Some people used ash or sugar to draw a dragon or snake on the ground and "led" it from the well (for drinking water) to the doorstep, and then from the doorstep to an urn in the house. This means the dragon had been brought into the house and, with a dragon in, the owner of the house was sure to get rich! In Shandong and Jiangsu provinces, ashes of burnt

Dragon legend.

wood and grass are used to draw large and small circles, one in the other; known as barn circles, they portend a good harvest. Some people also pile up ashes beside the barn circles in the shape of a ladder, implying that grains will be piled up mountain-high after a bountiful harvest.

The second day of the second month is a day in early spring, when all pests start to plague man and animal. So in some places, soy beans are fried with sugar on that day and, in other places, the Lantern Festival's left-over doughs are moulded into the shape of lamps and boiled. Both the fried beans, known as the "scorpion sting," and the boiled doughs are eaten with a view to avoiding the five poisonous things, namely, scorpion, snake, centipede, lizard and toad. In some parts of Jiangsu, New Year cakes left from the previous year, commonly known as "support the waist cake," are eaten to prevent, so people say, waist sores and help people work comfortably the year round. There is a poem dealing especially with this custom:

> *The second of the second month is a day in the best of*
> *the springtide.*
> *Eating on the day fancy cakes does one's waist good.*
> *A sound body is needed to bring home fuel and food*
> *By toiling without feeling tired the year round.*

In some parts of Hunan, people would fight shy of birds on that day. They would glue a certain sticky cake onto trees or place the cake in the field in the hope of catching birds and preventing them from destroying crops. In Fujian, it is the day for going to city outskirts and treading on greens.

Many folk customs are often tinged with superstition. With the spread of knowledge and science, such folk customs have gradually fallen into oblivion. On the contrary, healthy, festive celebrations, such as the display of dragon lanterns and rowing dragon boats, which prevail on the Spring Dragon Day thoroughout the country, will probably last.

4. Qingming Jie (Clear and Bright Festival)

Anecdotes About Qing Ming

Qing Ming has been one of the most popular festivities in China for thousands of years. People on that day go and pay respects to forebears at their tombs and go for outings. It is a day shortly after winter is over, a day in early spring, the season in which vegetation begins.

Qing Ming Festival is also known as Hanshi Jie, or the Day of Eating Things Cold. During the Spring and Autumn Period some two thousand years ago, Chong Er, son of Duke Xian of the State of Jin, was forced to live in exile in a foreign land for nineteen years. Most of his followers could not withstand the hardships any more and left him in the lurch. Only Jie Zitui and five or six others stuck to him loyally. When Chong Er wished to have some meat which was not available, Jie stealthily cut off some flesh from his own arm and cooked it for him to eat. Later, Chong Er became Duke Wen of the State of Jin with the help of Duke Mu of the State of Qin. To reward those who followed him throughout the exile according to their merits, he granted them titles and fiefs. Jie Zitui, however, after consulting with his mother, decided not to seek wealth and position but to live a secluded life in a mountain — Mianshan. Chong Er went personally to look for him but for several days running he could not find the mother and son. He knew Jie loved his mother dearly, calculating Jie would come out with his mother if he set the mountain on fire. But Jie would rather die than accept a reward for his meritorious deeds of the past. For three days and nights, the fire kept burning and finally reduced the whole place to ashes. Both Jie and his mother were found to have been burnt to death, their arms clinging to a scorched willow tree. Chong Er felt very sad and had Jie and his mother buried in the mountain, where a shrine was erected, and renamed the mountain after him in his memory. To remember forever Jie's loyalty for him, Chong Er had the scorched willow tree felled and brought back to make a pair of wooden shoes. Every day he would sigh at the shoes and lament: "Alas, the feet under!" Henceforth, in correspondence with a trusted friend, people in China like to begin a letter with "to so and so the feet under" as the salutation.

The day Duke Wen of Jin set fire on Mianshan happened to be the Qing Ming Festival. To pay him respects and in appreciation of the sterling quality of Jie Zitui, who would rather be burnt to death than be given a fief, people on that day put out their kitchen fire and eat cold things prepared beforehand. In time, this has become an accepted custom. This is also the day for people to sweep clean the tombs of their ancestors and mourn the dead.

Customs at the Festival

In ancient times, Qing Ming was the day for urban inhabitants, including women, to have an outing on the city outskirts, an affair known as *ta qing*, or treading on greens. Back from the outing, people would make garlands out of willow tree twigs and wear them on the head. Women would plait them into fine rings and pin them on the hair as a wish for their youth to stay forever. There was a saying: "Wearing no willow rings on the day of Qing Ming, a young woman will soon be growing grey."

Poets throughout the ages have from many views described the activities and sentiments on that day. There is one by the Tang Dynasty poet Du Mu:

> *It keeps raining in the Qing Ming season,*
> *Which makes a traveller on the road very sad indeed.*

> *Asked where could he find a wineshop,*
> *A cowherd points to a place in the distance — the Apricot*
>   *Blossoms Village!*

This custom of having an outing and paying respects to the deceased at the tomb is being observed to this day. In springtime, when the fields are green with life, it is the season for going outdoors, to the countryside to enjoy the beauty of the land. Paying respects to the deceased at the tombs on that day gives those who have survived an opportunity to meditate upon the martyrs who died for the Chinese revolution and on all forebears.

Kites

During the season, there are also various sports activities, such as playing on a swing, kicking a kind of ancient Chinese football, cockfighting, dog racing, flying kites and so on. The Tang Dynasty poet Wei Zhuang had a poem describing people enjoying a swing:

> *The street full of weeping willows whose branches are a*
>   *haze of green,*
> *What a picture of the Qing Ming Festival in an early month*
>   *of a year!*
> *Through a curtain blossoms on trees seem to be moving,*
> *When girls are aimlessly pushing the swinging seats to and*
>   *fro.*

Ancient China's football game originated from the Warring States Period; it used to be a very popular sport in the Tang and Song dynasties.

The tradition of flying kites is attributed to the Spring and Autumn Period more than two thousand years ago. There was a man named Gongshu Ban, who made a wooden bird and flew it at a high altitude to spy on the capital city of the State of Song. By the Western Han Dynasty, paper replaced wood in making

Clear and Bright Festival.

Kites.

this means of reconnaissance, an improvement made in 196 B.C. by Han Xin, an expert on military affairs, who used it to make surveys for military purposes.

By the time of the Five Dynasties, a man named Li Ye fixed a bamboo tube or a silk string on his paper kite so that it could not only ride the wind and fly up but also hover in the air. When the wind blew the bamboo tube, it produced a sound like the *zheng* (an ancient plucked instrument similar to the zither). Hence, *feng zheng* (wind instrument) has been the Chinese equivalent for kite in the past and present.

Kites as a pastime have undergone numerous changes in shape and structure in their continuous development. Every year before and after Qing Ming, when the weather is fine, people in threes and fives go to fly kites. Soon, kites of all descriptions fly in the blue sky, vying with each other in originality. Among these ingeniously designed kites are mythological characters, heroes in Chinese operas, butterflies flapping their wings and goldfish waggling their tails. There are also dragonflies, larks, bats, eagles, frogs and centipedes, which dart around the sky in a dazzling display. Many people have emerged as artisans technically superb in making kites and their products have become a unique Chinese craft of world fame.

"Riverside Scenes at Qing Ming"

Our story about Qing Ming will not be complete without mentioning *Riverside Scenes at Qing Ming*, the most outstanding scroll painting by Zhang Zeduan of the Northern Song Dynasty, an artist of the school of realism. The painting is now in the custody of the Palace Museum in Beijing. It vividly portrays life in Bianliang (now Kaifeng), the capital city of the Northern Song Dynasty, during the Qing Ming Festival. It begins with a few people paying respects to their dead kinsmen at the tombs on the city outskirts. This is followed by scenes along the banks of the Bianhe River, which is lined with budding willow trees suggesting spring at the Qing Ming Festival. Deep in the shade, there are mules and horse caravans coming all the way to the city from afar; in a village coolies are taking a rest by the roadside while some farmers are working in the field — all vividly life-like. As the river course gradually widens, the picture shows more people on the street and more boats on the river, some people towing boats, others loading or unloading ships. Big ships are at anchor side by side at a city-edge wharf, which presents the busiest scene in the painting. Under a bridge that spans the river like a rainbow, boatmen are busy at work. The river bank near the bridge is crowded with onlookers. There are restaurants and teahouses by the river, and the road is full of carts and people carrying things on shoulder-poles. Outside the city gate comes a caravan of camels, the beast of burden which connects water transport with land transport. Inside the city there are shops of different trades and human figures of all descriptions — an official on horseback, a lady in a sedan-chair, a local inhabitant in a red dress and some workmen. The number of human figures in the

Part of the famous Song Dynasty scroll painting
Riverside Scenes at Qing Ming.

painting is remarkable. There are 1,643 of them all told, plus 208 animals. Altogether there are over 20 ships and more than 20 carts and 30-odd buildings in the painting. It gives a picture of the industrial and commercial boom in the capital of the Northern Song Dynasty, portrays people's life and customs in those days and shows striking contrasts among people with different social backgrounds.

5. Duanwu Jie (Dragon Boat Festival)

Dragon's Day

Duanwu, or Duanyang, or Wuyue Jie (Fifth Month Festival), or Xia Jie (Summer Festival), is one of the three main folk festivities in China, apart from the Spring Festival and the

Mid-Autumn Festival. Duan Wu falls on the fifth day of the fifth lunar month and is an age-old festival. According to Wen yido, a noted contemporary scholar, this festival had been observed long before Qu Yuan (q.v.) was born and the many customs observed on that day had something to do with dragon. So Wen's conclusion was: "Duan Wu Festival... is the day for a tribe living in ancient Wu and Yue (now Jiangsu and Zhejiang) to offer sacrifices to its totem — the dragon. In short, it is a dragon's day." In recent years, there have been discoveries of cultural relics in Guangdong, Guangxi, Fujian, Taiwan, Zhejiang, Jiangsu, Anhui, Hunan and Hubei, relics consisting mainly of pottery and stone vessels with geometric markings on them. These relics, which can be dated back to a period between the late neolithic age and the pre-Qin and Han days, belonged to a tribe, which, with reference to historical legends and judging from the geographical locations, is most probably the tribe known in history as Baiyue, the tribe that worshipped the dragon as its totem. These people "cut their hair short and tattooed their bodies with dragons in such a way that they looked exactly like young dragons." They considered themselves scions of the dragon. So their festive day Duanwu Jie was actually a festive day of the dragons. With the fade-away of the totem culture, the old practice typical of a totem society, namely, bodies tattooed with dragons, gave way to the building of dragon boats. In other words, dragons were not only tattooed on one's body but drawn on things for use as well. Making *zong zi*, glutinous rice wrapped up in reed leaves, on the Dragon Boat Festival was originally done to offer to the dragon as a sacrifice. In many places in the country, there was the custom of collecting rain water on that day. It was supposed to be the holy water spread on earth by the heavenly dragon, and it had the reputation of preventing diseases. In some places, in ancient times, bronze mirrors with designs of crouched dragons on them were cast on a river on the festive day. With these mirrors on hand, it is said, rain would come if one prayed to heaven for it. From this we can readily see the change of the subject of worship in a primitive society. Men of the totem society in the pre-history era were at first so ignorant of and so helpless before the elements that they looked on the dragon as an almighty, supernatural being and worshipped it as such. By and by, with the advance of human society, man was able to find more effective means for controlling and transforming nature. With greater confidence in conquering nature, man gradually managed to break loose from the naive totem culture. By then, the festival as the day for worshipping the dragon totem, a rite originating in hoary antiquity, had lost its significance and was made a festival to honour the memory of China's great poet Qu Yuan of the Warring States Period.

In Commemoration of Qu Yuan

What is said above about the Duan Wu Festival in primaeval time, to a certain extent, is established folklore. But today it has been widely accepted that Duan Wu is the occasion to commemorate Qu Yuan.

During the Warring States Period some 2,300 years ago, there was a patriotic poet by the name of Qu Yuan, whose motherland was the State of Chu in the southern part of China. He was born in 340 B.C. (circa) at a time when Chinese society was in the throes of cataclysm. Frowning upon the corruptness of the aristocrats in the state, Qu proposed to effect domestic political reforms, set up a legal system and in civil service to employ only people of great competence and integrity. In affairs with other states, he advocated an alliance with the State of Qi in its confrontation with the State of Qin. This progressive stand he took was, however, opposed by the force of corruption represented by Jin Shang, aide of the King of Chu and Zheng

Xiu, the queen consort and the king's favourite. Both of them heaped calumnies on Qu Yuan and the King decided to banish him.

Qu Yuan, now at the wrong side of fifty, grief-stricken, left the capital Ying and wandered over the vicinity of Xiapu and Lingyang. With patriotic fervour he produced many odes showing his concern for his country and people. Among his masterpieces were *Li Sao* (*The Lament*), *Jiu Ge* (*Nine Odes*) and *Jiu Zhang* (*Nine Chapters*). There was a ring of sincerity in these verses, composed in a forceful way. They are a real treasure in Chinese and indeed world literature. In 278 B.C. the Qin troops stormed Ying and the downfall of the State of Chu was expected at any moment. Sixty-two-year-old Qu Yuan, holding a rock with both arms, drawned himself in the Miluo River near present-day Changsha, Hunan Province. He chose not to live and see his own country vanguished by the enemy.

Qu Yuan's quest for a way to make his country powerful and prosperous and his spirit of dedicating himself to his ideals had won the respect of the people. When the news of his death came, people rushed from all quarters to the scene, rowing boats on the river in an attempt to find his remains, which had drifted downstream and were never recovered. "People of Chu mourned his death and every year they threw bamboo tubes filled with rice into the river as a sacrifice offered to him." (See *Xu Qi Xie Ji*, or *More Strange Tales*) This is supposed to be the beginning of the custom of rowing dragon boats and eating *zong zi* on Duan Wu Day. The practice of planting Chinese mugwort leaves and calamus on doors during the festival is said to be a measure aimed at calling back Qu Yuan's soul.

That Qu Yuan is commemorated at the Duan Wu Festival signifies the popularity of a people's poet. Qu Yuan was among the four cultural giants the World Peace Council in 1957 called on the whole world to commemorate.

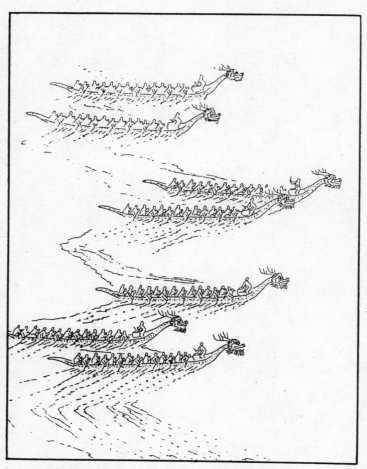
Dragon boat racing at the Dragon Boat Festival.

"Zong Zi"

Zong zi, glutinous rice wrapped up in reed leaves, is the traditional food eaten at the Duan Wu Festival. There is an interesting story about why rice is wrapped up this way. During the Eastern Han Dynasty, there lived in Changsha a native named Ou Hui, who one day chanced to see a man who called himself Minister in Charge of the Affairs of the Three Aristocratic Families (an official post once filled by Qu Yuan). "It is all very well for you to offer me sacrifices," said the man to Ou Hui, "but most of them were stolen and devoured by the dragon in the river. In future, please wrap them up in chinaberry leaves and tie them up with colour threads. The dragon is afraid of these two things and will never touch them." So people did as they were told and this is how *zong zi* is made in the way it is now.

Feng Tu Ji (*Notes on Local Customs*) by Zhou Chu of the Jin Dynasty spoke of "cooking triangular-shaped millet dumplings on Duan Wu in mid-summer." This millet dumpling is the very *zong zi* we know. The notes added that "millet is wrapped in wild rice leaves and boiled in a thick juice until it is well cooked, to be eaten on the fifth day of the fifth month and the Summer Solstice." Millet wrapped in these leaves and cooked in this kind of juice could not possibly taste good, nor could it look good or smell good. By the Tang and Song dynasties, there were all kinds of *zong zi* available. According to *Sui Shi Guang Ji* (*Miscellaneous Notes on Festive Occasions*), there were "*zong zi* in the shape of a triangle, a cone, a cylinder, or of a sliding weight (of a steelyard)...." All these were named after the shape in which the *zong zi* was made. The same book observed that "sugar or dates may be added in making *zong zi*; in recent years, pine seeds, chestnuts, walnuts, ginger, cassia, musk and the like may also be added." So it must taste far much better than the triangular millet *zong zi* in days of yore. In the Ming

Dynasty, *zong zi* was made in a very luxurious way. "Wash glutinous rice until it is clean, mix it with dates, chestnuts, dried persimmon, almond, red beans and wrap it with the leaves of bamboo or those of wild rice." (*Ming Gong Shi, or History of the Royal Household of the Ming Dynasty*) There was also the famous *zong zi* with Chinese mugwort flavour, for which the rice used was first soaked in water with mugwort leaves. By the Qing Dynasty, there were many different kinds of *zong zi*, each with a peculiar flavour, made in the south as well as in the north, in the royal kitchen and by the people of the common run. But the milk *zong zi* made in the royal kitchen of the Qing court must be considered the very best. The rice used was first soaked in cheese for a night before it was cooked. When making *zong zi* for the Duan Wu Festival, as many as several hundred catties of cheese were used.

Other *zong zi* worth mentioning include the ham *zong zi* of Yangzhou and *zong zi* wrapped in bamboo leaves — a southern speciality. As to fried mini-*zong zi* in the shape of water chestnut, it is really a "fare for immortals living in paradise"! (From *Yang Xiao Lu*, written in the Qing Dynasty) The stuffing for *zong zi* made in the Qing Dynasty was of great variety, including dates, sugar, lard, bean paste, fruit, assorted ingredients, rock candy, yam, haw, sesame and the traditional "five ingredients" including walnut and melon seeds.

In our time, *zong zi* made in Jiaxing, Ningbo, Suzhou and Guangdong Province and in Beijing are well known. Jiaxing *zong zi* is noted for its choice quality and excellent flavouring. Its ham *zong zi*, for instance, is made of quality rice soaked in soy sauce, and ham cubes mixed with sugar, wine and salt. Each *zong zi* contains a piece of fat meat sandwiched between two slices of lean meat. When cooked, the fat seeps into the rice so that the rice is oil rich but not greasy. Guangdong *zong zi* has a peculiar flavour of its own, stuffed with salted egg yolk, or assorted ingredients like chicken cubes, duck cubes, roast pork, egg yolk, mushroom or mung bean paste. Wrapped in lotus leaf, Guangdong *zong zi* is big in size, weighing about half a kilo each. Yellow rice *zong zi*, something special in north China, is sticky with a sweet smell. The Chinese people, while eating *zong zi* by way of commemorating the great patriotic poet Qu Yuan, have also created an artistic addition to their time-honoured culinary heritage.

6. Tiankuang Jie (Heaven's Gift Day)

Kuang means a gift and *tian kuang* means a gift from heaven. In the old days, every year on the sixth day of the sixth lunar month, Tiankuang Jie was observed in many parts of the country.

The festival began after the reunification of China by the First Emperor (Shi Huang Di) of the Qin Dynasty. He went to Taian in Shandong to offer sacrifices to heaven. The main hall in the Dai Temple on Taishan Mountain was made the site of the ritual. It was later named Tian Kuang Hall. Emperors of the succeeding dynasties all followed suit, making pilgrimages to Taishan Mountain at a specified date and offering sacrifices to heaven in the capacity of the self-assumed son of heaven.

In all these years, Tian Kuang Hall had been renovated again and again and it looked more magnificent after each renovation. The sixth day of the sixth month, too, became a festive day. In the Song Dynasty, Emperor Zheng Zong falsely said that he knew on the sixth day of the sixth month in a certain year, a book of heaven had fallen on earth and with it, "a wise ruler, an enlightened emperor," could govern the country

41

according to the will of heaven and the country would have peace and become affluent.

Buddhists, however, have their own story to tell about Tiankuang Jie. It was said that on his way home from the West in the early Tang Dynasty, some volumes of the scriptures Abbot Xuan Zang had brought back with him were wetted by sea water. They have been passed down to this day only after these volumes were sunned and dried after the accident. In Zhejiang, Buddhists had the custom of sunning scriptures. As time went on, scriptures are chanted instead of being sunned and in the evening of the fifth day of the sixth month, Buddhist disciples would assemble in temples to chant them.

Customs at the Festival

In Shandong Province, people eat wheat flour on that day. It is first baked and then mixed with hot water and eaten with sugar or salt. It may be eaten on that day or kept for consumption at a later date. Some people believe that eating baked flour that day may cure diarrhea. In Hebei, people on that day store up water for making yeast and brewing wine, which is said to be extremely mellow with an excellent bouquet.

The sixth day of the sixth lunar month is a day in summer swelteringly hot. In many places people have their clothing, bedding and books sunned on that day. In Hunan, while airing clothing and books under the sun, people also place clean water under sunshine for it to warm up for children to have bath in it. It is believed that this can prevent skin diseases. Some people on that day wash their horses and cattle in the hope that their animals will be immunized from disease.

Today, Tiankuang Jie as a festival and the superstitious ideas that go with it are gradually losing their significance in people's minds.

7. Qixi Jie (Double Seventh Night)

Starry Summer Night's Reverie

The seventh lunar month in China falls in hot summer. In the evening, people who have finished their day's work under the scorching sun will sit in their courtyard, waving a fan to cool themselves while looking up at the starry sky and telling fairy tales. Most of the tales are more or less related to stars. The night of the seventh day of the seventh month is called the Double Seventh Night and it is said that on this very night every year, Cowherd and Weaving Maid will walk across the bridge spanned by magpies for reuinion over the Heavenly River (the Milky Way). Yes, just look at the Milky Way overhead, white and steamy, dazzlingly bright — that's Weaving Maid crossing the Heavenly River for sure! But only those who are lucky will be able to see the scene and if they do and kneel down immediately to pray for wealth, a long life or a male issue, one of these three wishes — money, longevity or a son — will come true in three years. It is also said that when Weaving Maid is crossing the river, the Heavenly Gate is wide open, and if someone picks up a brick and throws it into the sky, it will turn into gold when falling down.

Cowherd and Weaving Maid

The story about Cowherd and Weaving Maid is so widely told that practically everyone, young and old, in this country knows it. It is also the very subject people talk about that evening. The earliest book which recorded the story is *Feng Su Tong* (*A Guidebook to Customs*) by Ying Shao of the Eastern Han Dynasty. It says: "On the night of the seventh day of the seventh month, Weaving Maid will cross the river, making the

43

magpies form a bridge for her." A more detailed record is found in the almanac *Yue Ling Guang Yi* under the chapter "The Seventh Month" compiled by Feng Yingjing in the Ming Dynasty. It says: "There lives a Weaving Maid, daughter of the Heavenly Emperor, at the eastern bank of the Heavenly River. Year in, year out, she works diligently at the shuttle and makes a heavenly garment of cloudy silk. She is so busy that she does not have time to take care of her appearance. The Heavenly Emperor, seeing that she is single and lonely, consents to her marrying Cowherd at the western bank. After marriage, however, she stops weaving altogether. The Heavenly Emperor gets angry and tells Weaving Maid to go back to the eastern bank but promises that the two may meet once every year."

The folklore of modern times about Cowherd and Weaving Maid is, however, better told. The story goes that Cowherd is an honest, upright and hardworking youth. As an orphan, he lives with his elder brother and sister-in-law, who is a very shrewd woman. She eventually forces him to leave their house and he is allowed to take away with him only a broken cart, an aged ox and two *mu** of barren land as his share of the property left by their parents. Cowherd now counts on the old ox to help him eke out a living and often calls it "Elder Brother the Ox." Now Elder Brother the Ox is sorry that the boy is single and promises to find him a wife. It confides to him that on a particular day in a particular month, there will be seven fairy girls coming down to the mundane world to play and take baths by the silvery river. If only he succeeds in snatching the cloth of any one of these fairy maids, she will marry him. Cowherd, following Elder Brother the Ox's advice, steals and brings home Weaving Maid's cloth in a misty moonlit night. The two become man and wife and are deeply in love. In three years, they

---

*1 *mu* = 1/15 hectare.

Cowherd reunites with Weaving Maid on the Double
Seventh Night.

Cowherd and Weaving Maid.

have a son and a daughter and live together happily. But this is found out by the Heavenly Emperor, who sends the Queen Mother of the Western Heaven to bring Weaving Maid back for a trial at the celestial court. The man and wife are separated. Cowherd, who cannot find a way to heaven, is grief-stricken. Elder Brother the Ox cannot bear to see the separation. It breaks one of its horns and transforms it into an ox-horn boat. Cowherd, together with his children, sails on the clouds in the boat to go after his wife. When he is about to catch up with her, the Queen Mother of the Western Heaven takes down a gold pin from her hair and uses it to draw a line in the air. Immediately a heavenly river with roaring waves appears in the sky. Cowherd and Weaving Maid, separated by the river, can only look at each other across it. Their true love deeply moves the kind-hearted phoenix, who calls in all the magpies in the universe to form a bridge over the river for the couple to cross and reunite on the evening of the seventh day of the seventh month. The legend has it that on that day, numerous bird feathers fall down from the sky because all the magpies have gone to form a bridge for Cowherd and Weaving Maid.

   The Altair and the Vega (known in this country as the

Cowherd Star and the Weaving Maid Star respectively) seen from the earth are separated by a "river" and it looks that the two are near enough to meet each other. But in astronomy, between the two stars is a distance of sixteen light years, or 150,000 billion kilometres. Even if Cowherd takes a spaceship flying at the speed of light, he will have to travel sixteen years for a reunion with Weaving Maid. This myth, nevertheless, tells of the harsh reality in feudal China in which men and women had no freedom in marriage. That the story ends with the man and wife meeting on a magpie bridge on the night of the seventh day of the seventh month nevertheless represents the wishes of the labouring people for a happier life.

Poems and Lyrics for the Double Seventh Night

The beautiful story about Cowherd and Weaving Maid has inspired countless men of letters of yesterday and today to write many meaningful, sentimental poems. The earliest and best among them is the classic ode *So Far Away Is Cowherd Star* carried in the *Wen Xuan* (*Selected Literary Pieces*) edited by Xiao Tong of the Liang Dynasty. The poem reads in full as follows:

> *So far away is Cowherd Star,*
> *So bright is Weaving Maid Star by the River.*
> *Using her soft, soft white hands,*
> *She works busily, busily with the shuttles in the loom.*
> *For a whole day, she cannot make a piece of beautiful cloth,*
> *Sobbing and weeping with tears trickling down like rainfall.*
> *Water in the River looks clear and shallow,*
> *But who knows how long one must travel in order to see each other?*
> *Separated by a stream,*

> *The two in love lack the means to communicate with each other.*

The lyric poem by Qin Guan of the Song Dynasty *The Clouds*, sung to the tune *Que Qiao Xian*, is really a masterpiece with love as its theme. The poet's emotions in the lyric poem are genuine, the words used are sincere and the verses are beautifully written. A tentative English translation reads as follows:

> *The clouds are changing patterns in an ingenuous way,*
> *Separated by the Milky Way,*
> *The two air their sorrows of separation.*
> *Crossing the broad river stealthily,*
> *They can only meet once a year in a breezy, dewy night.*
> *And yet the moment's reunion is so much sweeter than trysts*
>   *on earth!*
> *The gentle emotions are smooth as water,*
> *The rendezvous as transitory as a dream.*
> *Soon they will have to part again,*
> *Sadly looking at the way back over the magpie bridge!*
> *But if the love between them is said to be everlasting,*
> *It may not matter much if they cannot be together day and*
>   *night, night and day!*

"Will I Be Clever?"

The Weaving Maid in legend is a good hand at weaving. The Double Seventh Night is also known among girls as the day to find out if they will be clever or not. This means it is the day for girls to beg Weaving Maid to give them a pair of nimble hands. In ancient times, there were two different ways of "begging for nimble hands." One was to ask through divination if one was clever or clumsy with one's hands. The way to do it is put a small spider in a box to see if it makes a web the next

47

day, and if it does, to see whether it is closely or loosely knit and whether it is well-shaped or not. A closely knit, well-shaped web foretells cleverness. The other way is known as "seeking cleverness." "In the sixth lunar month, soak sweet peas or mung beans in well water, sealed and kept away from light. Change water once every several days until the seventh day of the seventh month when the sprout has grown about one foot high. Tie the sprout with a band of red paper at its middle part." The girl concerned, having prostrated before the two stars of Cowherd and Weaving Maid, breaks the sprout by hand about several *fen* (1 *fen* = 1/3 cm.) in length, and throws it in a basin of clear water. The next day before sunrise, she goes to see if the reflection of the sprout at the bottom of the basin is tapered and lengthy like a needle. If it is, it means she will be clever and have a pair of nimble hands. It is said that on the Double Seventh Night, when all is quiet, a young woman may hide herself by a well or under a grapevine and hold her breath and listen. If she succeeds in hearing however vaguely the whispers between Cowherd and Weaving Maid, she will be clever with a pair of nimble hands. In some places, the Double Seventh Night is simply referred to as the "Women's Day." On that night, they will get together and hold a needlework contest. Before the contest begins, they will spread melons and other fruit on a dinner table to offer to the two stars as sacrifices. They will then each start putting coloured threads into the holes of nine needles. The one finishing first wins, and the winner is supposed to be the cleverest among them all.

8. Zhongyuan Jie (Middle of the Year Festival)

According to an old Chinese custom, the fifteenth day of the first lunar month is Shangyuan Jie (Upper Part of the Year Festival), or Yuanxiao Jie (Lantern Festival); the fifteenth day of the seventh month is Zhongyuan Jie (Middle of the Year Festival) and the fifteenth day of the tenth month Xiayuan Jie (Lower Part of the Year Festival). Zhongyuan Jie is actually a Buddhist festival.

There are a number of stories which differ as to the origin of the festival. One story says it is the birthday of Sakyamuni, founder of Buddhism. He was said to be born on the fifteenth day of the seventh month in the year Kui Chou (see Appendix 2); his mother was Mahamaya, wife of the King Suddhodana. Another story says that an envoy of the nether world will come on that day to this world to find out how people here behave, whether they have sinned or performed good deeds. Only by asking Taoist priests to chant scriptures day and night can the hungry ghosts suffering tortures in the nether world be spared by the envoy. A more popular story is about a deity named Mu Lian, whose mother after death is unfortunately sent where ghosts are starved. Anything a ghost there puts into her mouth goes up into raging flames and so she cannot eat at all. To deliver his mother from this suffering, Mu Lian leaves his home to seek the help of Buddha, who imparts to him a whole volume of *Ullambana Sutra*, the sutra that will save people from "hanging by the feet," that is, from bad times. It is said that by chanting this sutra, all deities from four corners will be called in to come to the rescue of Mu Lian's mother. So Mu Lian chants the sutra on that day.

Based on this story, rich people who believed in Buddhism and the principle that "to be dutiful to one's parents is the very first good deed one may perform," often asked monks and nuns to chant the sutra that day in the hope that their parents in the other world may not suffer. A Buddhist altar would be set up together with a table on which an incense burner and offerings are placed for the priests to chant *Ullambana Sutra* for the deceased, for the parents and forebears seven generations past. Alms would be given away to the monks and nuns and to the poor in remembrance of the donor's parents. Many people would go and pay respects to ancestors at the tombs, burning paper money or tinfoil paper by way of mourning. Sutra is also chanted on that day solely for the purpose of comforting the starved or lonely ghosts everywhere. So this day is also called the "Ghost Festival." It may be said that among China's folk customs, those observed on Zhongyuan Jie are the most superstitious by nature.

The chanting of *Ullambana Sutra* soon developed into a rite at which sutra is chanted in day time and lanterns are floated on a river in night time. In south China in the Ming Dynasty, thirty-six lamps were lit and floated on a river on the festive night. These lamps were, it is said, to give a helping hand to the homeless ghosts. Similar custom also prevailed in Yunnan. On this day of the month, every family would make some lotus flower lamps and leave them at roadside or on water to "light the way for the wronged ghosts to get reincarnated in a new body." If a lamp sank into the river, it meant the lamp had been picked up by a wronged ghost; if it remained afloat, it meant there were no wronged ghosts around. Lamps were made in the shape of wild geese, fish, tortoises and the like and were thrown into water as offerings to deities. In a moonlit early autumn night, ghosts or no ghosts, deities or no deities, when many tiny lamps were glistening and moving on a river, it must have been a wonderful sight.

In Shaanxi, peasants assemble and drink wine in the festive night. They call this "hanging up the hoe." Or, they may hang up five-coloured pennants over a piece of land on which crops are growing well. They call these pennants "the field pennant," which is a symbol of good harvest. In Jiangsu, in that night, papers of different colours are cut like flower petals and stuck on the brim of a bowl with oil for lighting — this is known as "the candle of Ksitigarbha." In Chaoan, Guangdong Province, there goes a story about a big landlord named Xu, who bullied local inhabitants and provoked the peasants to revolt. They secretly made the fifteenth day of the seventh month the day for an uprising when the Ullambana Rite was taking place. Divided into nine groups, the insurgents killed many local despots and members of the tyrannical gentry. But the revolt was eventually brutally suppressed. In memory of those innocent people killed in the turmoil, peasants in the locality burn incense every year on that day.

9. Zhongqiu Jie (Mid-Autumn Festival)

Why Mid-Autumn?

Every year the fifteenth day of the eighth lunar month is the Mid-Autumn Festival in China. Why is it so called? According to ancient calendar system, the eighth lunar month is in the middle of the autumn season (the seventh, eighth and ninth months making up the autumn season) and the fifteenth day of the eighth month is in the middle of that month (it having thirty days). This is why it is called the Mid-Autumn Festival. On that night, the moon is supposed to be brighter and fuller than in any other month and the moonlight is the most beautiful. In China a full moon is also symbolic of family reunion and so that day is also known as the "day of reunion."

It is a grand occasion because there are myths and legends galore about the moon. The most popular one is about Chang E who flies to the moon. In remote antiquity, it is said, there were ten suns shining simultaneously in the sky. "The sunshine was hot like fire and the four seas were boiling, mountains falling and the earth cracking. All plant life was scorched and burnt." People had no place for shelter. Then, a man named

Hou Yi, thanks to his valour and marksmanship, opened his bow and shot down nine suns in a stretch. Only one sun was left. He had thus helped the people to avert the disaster. He was respected and loved by the people, who made him the king. After he became the king, however, he began to indulge in wine and women, killing people as he liked and making himself a tyrant hated by everyone. Aware that his days were numbered, he went to the Fairy Queen Mother Wang Mu on Kunlun Mountain for some elixir. His wife Chang E, who did not wish him to live forever and bring havoc to the people, swallowed the elixir herself. Immediately, she found wind blowing under her feet and herself light as cloud. Before long she was flying in the air. It was already late in the night and the moon was shining. She had always liked moonlight and said to herself it would be nice to fly to the Moon Palace and stay there for a while. No sooner had she had the idea than she found herself landed on the moon. In the Moon Palace she met an old man, who called himself Wu Gang, sent there to fell a cassia tree as a punishment for the mistakes he had made in the course of his studies to become an immortal. But the opening on the tree closed immediately after he withdrew his axe and so he had to keep on falling, falling. . . .

When man's knowledge about nature was very rudimentary and when he could not explain the shadow on the moon, he invented one story after another to give vent to his well-intentioned imagination. Because of these interesting legends, we feel the Mid-Autumn Festival is all the more poetic, enchanting and picturesque.

Moon Worship

It is a national custom to offer sacrifice to the moon at the Mid-Autumn Festival. In remote antiquity, the primitive tribes would dance and celebrate good harvest on a moonlit night and

Moon worship at the Mid-Autumn Festival.

by bonfires. This could be the harbinger of the rite to offer sacrifices to the moon. From early historical records, people in the Jin Dynasty developed the custom of worshipping the moon by prostration and revelling under moonlight throughout the night. In the succeeding dynasties, emperors too made it a rule to offer sacrifices to the moon on that night, a ritual praying for a good harvest amidst music. Celebrations at the festival became increasingly colourful as time went on. It was probably in the Northern Song Dynasty that the Mid-Autumn Festival was marked by the people at large as their own festivity. According to *Dongjing Menghua Lu (Memoirs of the Eastern Capital)*, Dongjing (or Eastern Capital, in present-day Kaifeng), capital city of the Northern Song Dynasty, was especially bustling with activity on the night of the Mid-Autumn Festival. The facades of wineshops selling aged vintage wine on that day were all freshly painted and their entrances decorated with festoons and lanterns. Fruit shops were, of course, overflowing with fruit in season and the evening market did a very brisk business. Tables at practically all wineshops were reserved beforehand by those wishing to see moonlight while nursing a cup of wine.

When night fell, with the moon shining overhead and a gentle breeze bringing people a cool air filled with the sweet odour of cassia blossoms, it must have been a very wonderful experience. Thousands upon thousands of families had a table placed in the courtyard under the moon, on which incense was burned and fruit of all varieties in season were spread. There were also cooked soy beans, peanuts seasoned with spices, and taroes. At the centre was a big moon cake cut into a number of slices equal to the number of people in the family. A stem of fresh soy bean — considered as the cassia tree in the moon — was to be planted in the incense burner. When everything was in ship shape order, everyone in the family would prostrate before the moon in turn. Worshipping the moon actually meant paying

53

respcts to Chang E who allegedly lives in the Moon Palace; Chang E is believed to be a female and the moon is supposed to be a she, so generally a woman would preside over the ritual. After the ritual, the whole family would sit together in a circle, eating the offerings and chatting. The elderly people would start telling children the legendary tales of the Moon Palace and the listeners often glued their eyes to the story-teller, spellbound.

Every year the emperors of the Ming and Qing dynasties supervised the ritual of worshipping the moon. The ritual observed by Empress Dowager Ci Xi of the Qing Dynasty was especially elaborate and unprecedented in scale. That night, followed by court officials and escorted by ladies-in-waiting, the Empress Dowager presided over the ritual at Pai Yun (Dispelling the Clouds) Hall in the Summer Palace. The offerings, apart from the choicest moon cakes, lotus roots with seven joints and all kinds of fruit, included a "moon flower" (*yue hua*) specially made by the royal chef with a diameter of several feet. (The royal family did not use the term *yue bing* (moon cake), because the word sickness is also pronounced as *bing*. So they preferred to call it *yue hua* instead.) On the cake were carved designs of Guang Han Gong (Vast and Cold Moon Palace), the cassia tree and Chang E. The offerings also included a big watermelon, cut by the best royal chef into several pieces but not yet off the base so that it looked like a big water lily in full bloom. This was named "water lily melon for grand reunion." It was placed in a big bronze plate made also in the shape of a water lily. After the ritual, the huge moon cake was cut into small slices and, together with the melon, was distributed as an imperial favour among the royal concubines in the harem, eunuchs and palace maids. The emperor and the queen would then embark on a dragon boat, accompanied by retinues in other boats, and float on Kunming Lake for pleasure. Delicacies were served on board, known as "banqueting and boating by imperial favour." Over the lake, fireworks were displayed; on the lake floated water lily lanterns....

Yue Tan (Moon Altar) Park outside Fuchengmen Gate in Beijing was the old site for emperors to worship the moon; it was built in the ninth year of Jia Jing (1530) of the Ming Dynasty. The main building there was an altar for offering sacrifices to the moon. There are also annexes, installations and facilities for the purpose, such as a bell tower, a hall for changing clothes, the storage for keeping sacrificial utensils, the pavilion for slaughtering animals as sacrifices and the kitchen for cooking them.

Moon Cake

In China, people eat something special on a particular traditional festival. They eat, for instance, steamed cake on the Double Ninth Day. The moon cake for the Mid-Autumn Festival, round in shape, is also called "reunion cake."

People began making moon cakes in the Tang Dynasty and it became a very popular pastry in the Song Dynasty. "Moon cake as an offering to the moon was available everywhere. The big ones are over one foot in diameter, with carvings of the Moon Palace and the Moon Rabbit on them. Some people ate it after the sacrificial ceremony while others kept it until the New Year Eve." (*Yanjing Suishi Ji*, or *Memoirs of the Festive Days in Beijing*: "The Moon Cake") Su Dongpo of the Song Dynasty in a poem wrote:

A small piece of cake to eat as if crunching the moon;
Tasting like shortbread with maltose inside.

In the Ming Dynasty, it was a custom for people to exchange moon cakes by way of greeting at a family reunion. In the Qing

Dynasty, the moon cake was well stuffed with walnut paste. So the moon cake of that time was more or less the same as the one we now have. The ways of making moon cakes vary from place to place and so their flavours are also not the same, each with something special. Those made in Suzhou are like shortbread with several layers containing gingko, bean paste, spiced salt, or pork. Those made in Beijing are made with vegetable oil and vegetable stuffing. The moon cakes of Chaozhou are oily and very sweet. Those of Guangzhou are oil-rich and look good, with a large quantity of stuffing inside a very thin dough. The stuffings are cocoanut paste, lotus seed paste, assorted fruit seeds and nuts, egg yolk, chicken, ham, or cassia and date paste. Moon cakes sell like wildfire during the festival.

Different customs are observed at different places. In some places, people go and see the beautiful sight of cassia blossoms at the Mid-Autumn Festival; in other places, they have a family reunion dinner, drink sweetened wine, and eat lotus roots and water chestnuts; at still other places, people display fancy lanterns and sing folk songs. The Mid-Autumn Festival is generally accepted as an occasion for family reunion. So on that day, a married woman who has been staying with her parents must go back and join her husband and the rest of his family.

Moon Poetry

The moon has always been looked on as the symbol of brightness, purity and goodness by men of letters in ancient times. Chinese poets of the previous ages had left us many beautiful odes to the moon. Du Fu, to express the sentiments of a man living in a strange land and getting homesick, wrote:

> *White will be the dews from tonight on,*
> *Bright is the moon over my native place.*

Wang Anshi, with a feeling of nostalgia, wrote:

*Now that the wind of springtime has again turned trees in
Jiangnan* green with life,
I wonder when the moon will light up my way home.*

Li Bai had the moon personified in one of his poems:

*I raise my wine cup and ask the Moon to join me in a drink,
Facing my own shadow there are three of us now.*

The lyric poem sung to the tune *Shui Diao Ge Tou* by Su
Shi is a masterpiece without parallel. The last two lines are
couched with such optimism and open-mindedness that they
make readers feel inspired and filled with a sense of
contentment:

*And so let us, a thousand miles apart, live long,
And together enjoy this beautiful moon.*

Some music, like poetry, has the moon as the leitmotif. The
ancient *qin* (seven-stringed plucked instrument) music *Moon
over Guanshan Mountain*, the Cantonese music *Reflections of
the Moon in Three Pools* and *Reflections of the Moon in Two
Fountains* by the late folk musician Ah Bing are some instances
of such music.

10. Chongyang Jie (Double Ninth Day)

Story About the Festival

The ninth day of the ninth lunar month is the traditional
Chong Yang Festival of the Chinese people. In ancient times,
people regarded nine as a *yang* (positive or masculine) numeral

---

*A loose geographical term for places in east China south of the Changjiang
(Yangtze River).

standing for good luck, happiness and a bright future.

This particular day with two *yang* numerals—a *yang* day in a *yang* month—is called *chong yang* (double *yang* or double ninth). *Jiu jiu* (nine nine) in Chinese is pronounced the same as the word "long, long" is pronounced, which means everlasting peace. People in this country have all along appreciated the dual meaning of *jiu jiu*. In the Ming and Qing dynasties, for example, the imperial palace had 9,999 rooms. Chong Yang was marked as a festive day as early as the Eastern Han Dynasty about two thousand years ago.

In the Eastern Han Dynasty, there was a man from Runan named Huan Jing, who was the disciple of a Taoist priest called Fei Zhangfang. One day, Fei warned his disciple that "disaster will visit your home on the ninth day of the ninth month. Tell everyone in your family at once to make a red pouch with the fruit of a cornel plant in it, tie it round the arm, go and climb up a mountain and drink some chrysanthemum wine there. This way you may be able to get away from the disaster." The red pouch mentioned here was made of gauze and was called a "fragrance pouch" when it was filled with cornel fruit. So on that day Huan Jing and his family did as Fei told them. Later, when he and his family came back home from the mountain, they found all their domestic animals were dead. Since then, wearing cornel fruit, drinking chrysanthemum wine and climbing up a mountain have become customs that guard against evils and avert disasters.

By the Tang Dynasty this had already become a very popular practice. People often got together with friends to drink wine and write poems. Sometimes, even the emperor would personally attend such festive activities. Tang Emperor Zhong Zong (Li Xian) took the lead by dining on a terrace with his guests while writing poems. Du Fu, known as the sage poet, also went up to a mountain on a Double Ninth Day even when he was sick. Other Tang Dynasty poets like Meng Haoran and Wang Wei both have left us odes to the Double Ninth Day.

Customs at the Festival

About wearing cornel plant, there is a passage in *Feng Tu Ji* (*Notes on Local Customs*) by Zhou Chu: "Cornel plant is plucked on the ninth day of the ninth month and worn on the head to dispel evil air and resist the incipient cold weather." Cornel is a kind of evergreen shrub blossoming in late spring and early summer and bearing fruit in autumn. Its fruit is used as a medicinal substance or to make wine that keeps one's body warm while assuaging pain caused by functional disorders of various organs. Its leaf has a curative effect against cholera and its root may serve as insecticide. When one carries cornel with him, no mosquito will sting him.

Watching chrysanthemum flower on the Double Ninth Day is a delight. Chrysanthemum flowers, known in China also as the yellow flower, with multifarious strains, have a light sweet odour and bloom in spite of cold, frosty weather. Even when the flowers have faded and fallen off, the stem remains erect. Watching chrysanthemum flowers on the Double Ninth Day is an age-old custom. Meng Yuanlao in his book *Memoirs of the Eastern Capital* gave an account of the spectacular event of "people of the capital watching chrysanthemum flowers on the Double Ninth Day" in the Northern Song Dynasty. The Qing Dynasty had in some parts of the country chrysanthemum flower shows round the time of the Double Ninth, generally held once very three to five or ten years. The chrysanthemum flower show taking place once in every sixty years (each sixty years in the Chinese calendar system is a cycle) was an especially grand occasion. It is said that if one lived to see two chrysanthemum flower shows in two sixty-year cycles, his cup of happiness was full. At these flower shows, where thousands of chrysanthemum flowers were on display, people would admire them, poets would write odes to them and artists would draw pictures of them on the spot. Today, there are still chrysanthemum flower shows in some parts of the country. Ornamental chrysanthemum flowers include green and blue ones while there are some chrysanthemum flowers that are used to make drinks or medicine.

Drinking chrysanthemum wine was another custom in ancient China. "People today put chrysanthemum flowers and cornel in wine and drink it." (*Meng Liang Lu*, or *Notes by Wu Zhimu*) Chrysanthemum flower wine is good for one's eyes, and helps bring down blood pressure.

Double Ninth comes in the middle of the autumn season. The weather at that time is neither hot nor cold. The sky is often cloudless. Maple leaves have turned crimson and chrysanthemum flowers are in full bloom. It is time for an outing. Here in China, people still work six days a week and have only one day, Sunday, off. Although the Double Ninth may not fall on a Sunday, one can always spend a holiday round the Double Ninth climbing a mountain, or boating, or enjoying the beautiful sights of chrysanthemum and cassia flowers.

Odes to Chrysanthemums

Ancient Chinese poets had had many odes to chrysanthemum flowers, odes that are genuinely emotional, oft-quoted and widely loved. Tao Yuanming of the Jin Dynasty, who, as he himself had made it clear in prose, "refused to bow to the superior merely for an emolument of five *dou* (a unit of dry measure) of rice," had written verses on chrysanthemum flowers like the following:

> *Plucking chrysanthemum flowers under a fence at the east side,*

> *I catch the sight of the mountain at the south side.*
> *Chrysanthemum flowers in autumn look so very wonderful,*
> *I scoop up the dew on them to get their very essence.*

His pastoral poetry speaks volumes for his upright personality.

Cen Can, a Tang Dynasty poet living at a frontier region, wrote a poem entitled "The Nine-Day March Took My Thoughts Back to the Garden in My Changan Residence":

> *On ascending a height I insist,*
> *No one is there to bring me wine.*
> *Alas, how I miss the chrysanthemums in the garden of my*
> *   former residence!*
> *They should have bloomed right here by the battlefield.*

Huang Chao, leader of the peasant insurgents at the end of the Tang Dynasty, expressed novel ideas in an ode to chrysanthemum flowers. He wrote:

> *Wait till the eighth or ninth month when autumn comes,*
> *When my flower is in bloom after a hundred other flowers*
> *   have withered away,*
> *When it scents the air of Changan*
> *And the whole city is swarmed with my soldiers in golden*
> *   armours.*

The lyric poem on chrysanthemum by Mao Zedong is instilled with lofty sentiments peculiar to him:

> *Man ages all too easily, not Nature:*
> *Year by year the Double Ninth returns.*
> *On this Double Ninth,*
> *The yellow blooms on the battlefield smell sweeter.*

> *Each year the autumn wind blows fierce,*
> *Unlike spring's splendour,*
> *Yet surpassing spring's splendour,*
> *See the endless expanse of frosty sky and water.*

11. Laba Jie (Eighth Day of the Twelfth Month)

A Vestige of Hoary Antiquity

The twelfth lunar month is called the month of *la* and the eighth day of the month of *la* is called the day of *ba*.

La means all in one. In ancient times, people used to offer sacrifices to heaven and earth, to deities and forebears all at once during the interval between the outgoing year and the forthcoming year. This was known as "*la* worship." Some people are of the opinion that *la* (the word hunting is pronounced similarly to *la*) here means people piously offering the game they had hunted to their forebears—a vestige of ancestral worship in a primitive society.

Activities of the common folks on the day of *la* in ancient times were recorded in *Jingchu Shuishi Ji* (*New Year's Day and Other Festive Occasions in Jingchu* [now Hubei] by Liang Zhonglin of the Southern Song Dynasty: "The eighth day of the twelfth month is the day of *la*. There is a saying: 'When drums are beaten on the day of *la*, it means spring has set in for grass to grow again.' Villagers would beat waist drums, put on masks to appear as foreigners or disguise themselves as Vajra (Buddhist deity) for the purpose of chasing epidemics out of reach." It is the old belief that disguising oneself as Vajra or other deities and dancing and beating drums on the day of *ba* or the day before it may avert disasters and drive away devils.

A Buddhist Festival

The La Ba Festival is a day for the Buddhists. In the past in places where the Han people lived, it was believed to be the day Sakyamuni attained immortality. So on that day, scriptures were chanted at monasteries and festive rice congee was prepared as offerings to Buddha. There is an interesting anecdote about the *la ba* rice congee: It says that the Buddhist founder Sakyamuni had visited many mountains and rivers in India before he became the Buddha, meeting abbots and men of unusual calibre in quest of the true meaning of life. When he came near a river in the State of Magadha (now Bihar State) in northern India, because of the heat and because he was exhausted and hungry, he collapsed and fell on the ground in a deserted place. At that time there came a shepherdess, who fed him with her own lunch and water she had drawn up from a fountain and heated. The lunch was actually a hodgepodge of leftovers in her family kitchen for the last few days. It consisted of all kinds of sticky cereals, glutinous rice, dates, wild chestnuts and wild fruit she had collected on the mountain slope. However, it was better than anything to Sakyamuni, who had not had anything to eat for many days. After the meal, he had a bath in the river and sat under a pipal tree for meditation. Then he became Buddha on the eighth day of the twelfth month. Since then, every year on that day, monks assemble to chant scriptures and give lectures on Buddhism, and eat sticky rice congee to mark the occasion.

La Ba Congee

Monks in China have been eating *la ba* rice congee for more than one thousand years. It first began in the Song Dynasty. The book *Tian Zhong Ji* says that on the eighth day of the twelfth month in the capital of the Northern Song Dynasty, all monasteries there gave away "congee with seven ingredients and five flavours," known as *la ba* congee. It was made not only by the royal household, government offices and monasteries, but also by ordinary families. By the Qing Dynasty, eating *la ba* congee became a widespread custom. The emperor, the queen and princess would all bestow congee on ministers and army officers, attendants and palace maids and issue rice and fruit to the various leading monasteries so the monks there could make and eat *la ba* congee. There, monks would hold a religious service at which scriptures were chanted in memory of Sakyamuni. The average lay men everywhere too made *la ba* congee on that day to celebrate bountiful harvest.

Fucha Dunchong of the Qing Dynasty in his book *Memoirs of the Festive Days in Beijing* gave a detailed account of how to prepare *la ba* congee: "*La ba* congee is a mixture of yellow and white rices, glutinous rice, millet, water chestnut, chestnut, red beans and date paste. It is cooked in water, spread with walnut, then dyed in red, with almond, melon seed, peanut, pine seed, hazelnut, sugar and raisin for decorative effects. Every year on the seventh day of the twelfth month, people crack nuts and clean the utensils, making preparations for the whole night. By dawn the congee is ready. It will be used first as offerings to ancestors and the Buddha and then given to relatives and friends not later than noon time. "In making *la ba* congee, a greater variety of ingredients are preferred," for people "were even more enthusiastic than the ancients in trying to prepare [*la ba* congee] of the best quality." This was how people marked the festival in the Qing Dynasty. Today people still eat *la ba* congee on that day but only as the season's speciality having nothing to do with Sakyamuni.

Inhabitants in and near Beijing often pickle garlic in vinegar in a sealed bottle at this time of the year. The bottle would not be opened until the Spring Festival; the vinegar would have the taste of garlic and the garlic the good smell of vinegar.

12. Jizao Jie (Kitchen God's Day)

Origin of the Rite

On the twenty-third day of the twelfth lunar month there is

in China the custom of offering sacrifices to the Kitchen God, one that dates back two to three thousand years.

The Kitchen God was said to be a deity in charge of cooking and fuel in the mundane world. Its idol, placed on the kitchen range, was also known as the Kitchen Deity or Kitchen King. A description of the Kitchen God can be found in the classic novel *Feng Shen Bang* (*Canonization of the Gods*). He was, in fact, not merely in charge of cooking and fuel but an "envoy" of the Jade Emperor in heaven to the mundane world. He would record from time to time people's merits and misdeeds and went back to the Palace in Heaven every year on the twenty-third day of the twelfth month to report to the Jade Emperor. Thus, people in this country who believed the existence of deities dared not offend him and always respected him as "master of the household" in the hope that he would "put in a good word for them when in heaven and bless them when on earth." On that day, every family made offerings of sugar and fruit to the Kitchen King, who was said to be going back to heaven for consultations. A "horse" made of sorghum stem was ready for the Kitchen King to ride on his journey; crushed husks were provided as the "horse's" fodder and a bowl of water for the "animal." The Kitchen King was respectfully removed from the kitchen range and burnt together with candles, incense, tinfoil paper, the "horse" and the fodder, which meant that the Kitchen God was now on his way to heaven. He would be welcomed home again on the New Year Eve by buying a new portrait of the Kitchen King and having it pasted on the kitchen range. Because people do not speak of *buying* a Kitchen God, which was profanity, they often used the word "welcome" or "invite" instead.

Legends About the Kitchen King

Who is the Kitchen King? The answer is not the same if one

Kitchen God and Kitchen Goddess.

refers to different sources. According to a book entitled *You Yang Za Zu* (*Miscellaneous Notes*), the Kitchen King's family name is Zhang. This has long been taken for granted, probably because Zhang is the surname of the Jade Emperor in heaven and the Kitchen King, as his subordinate, might as well have come from the same family.

Whatever the surname, that the Kitchen King is a male deity is beyond dispute. This is why generally it was a man who would preside over the rite of offering sacrifices to him. In north China, people used to say "a man never prostrates to worship the Moon and a woman should not be the one to offer sacrifices to the Kitchen King." But we must not ignore the fact that beside our Kitchen King, there is always the Kitchen Queen with a kindly face.

66

According to a legend, long, long ago, there was a young man named Zhang, who was married to a virtuous, dignified-looking woman, Guo Dingxiang (Lilac) by name. The husband worked in the field and the wife at a loom. In less than three years, they accumulated a big fortune. Soon Zhang took a woman named Haitang (Crabapple) as his concubine. She was a jealous woman, who was lazy and liked to enjoy life. Infatuated by her beauty, Zhang soon deserted his wife Lilac. He and Crabapple lived a life of dissipation and in less than two years they had squandered all their money and became penniless. Crabapple, who loathed living in poverty, left Zhang and married someone else. Soon Zhang became a beggar. In a snowy, windy day, starved and cold, he broke down in front of a house at its doorstep. A housemaid found him and brought him into the kitchen and let him warm himself up and eat his fill. Zhang was very grateful for this and asked the name of her master. The maid told him her mistress was a kind-hearted widowed lady without any kith and kin. At this, the mistress appeared and Zhang could recognize that she was none other than the Lilac he had jilted two years before. He was so ashamed of himself that he crawled into the stove chamber trying to hide himself. When the maid pulled him out, Zhang was already dead. Lilac, recognizing that the man was her ex-husband, was quite sad and upset. Unhappy, she too died a few days later.

Earlier, when the Jade Emperor heard of Zhang's betrayal he had intended to punish him severely for his being unfaithful to his wife. But since Zhang had later realized his wrong doing and had been burnt to death in the stove chamber, the Jade Emperor changed his mind and, instead, made Zhang the Kitchen God and Lilac the Kitchen Goddess, and let the couple have a place at people's kitchen ranges and be worshipped forever by people of the mundane world.

The Custom

Although the custom of offering sacrifices to the Kitchen God is a time-honoured one, the offerings were rather meagre — maybe Kitchen King Zhang, once spendthrift and later penniless, knew very well the straits the poor people were in and therefore did not expect too much from them. Luo Ying, a Tang Dynasty poet, once wrote:

> *Served a cup of tea and a column of smoke [incense]*
> *His Majesty the Kitchen King goes up to the blue sky.*

So all the Kitchen King could enjoy at that time was just a cup of tea, he being less demanding of the religious people than any other deities in legend. Later, because people knew their sacrifices were too mean and for fear that the "envoy from heaven" would be offended, they added a kind of malt sugar to the offerings to the Kitchen King. This may not amount to much, but it had the advantage of sticking up the Kitchen King's teeth. Of course, people weren't worrying about the Kitchen Queen because she was such a nice lady and she wouldn't mind even if they had sinned once or twice in a year or even snubbed her. But they were not quite sure about the Kitchen King, so it would be better for them to seal up his mouth with malt sugar in the hope that he would discreetly keep his mouth shut when he went back to heaven.

Offering sacrifices to the Kichen King as a custom is still being observed in China on the twenty-third day of the twelfth month. But now, it is just a matter of distributing malt sugar among the kids who will chew it with relish. As to the rite of sending off the Kitchen God to his heaven, people now no longer bother about it.

13. Chuxi Jie (New Year Eve)

New Year Eve Dinner

The last evening of the twelfth lunar month is the New Year Eve, or *Chu Xi*. *Chu* means getting rid of and *xi* means night. So *Chu Xi* means the night to get rid of an old year and usher in a new one.

The whole family will invariably get together that evening for a reunion dinner. In north China, the dinner means dumplings and in the south a very sumptuous feast. In Shaoxing, Zhejiang Province, it has ten courses. One speciality served is asparagus lettuce soaked in rice water to soften, fried in oil and again stewed with soy sauce and vinegar, and cooked again with lotus root, gingko, dates and brown sugar. This lotus root (*ou*) and the other additives (*cou*), that is, the combination of the two words, mean in Chinese turning ill luck into good luck. For New Year Eve dinner in Hangzhou, Suzhou and Shanghai, egg dumplings are a must because they are made in the shape of *yuan bao*, a silver or gold ingot. Made of golden yellow egg sheets, they are stuffed with red minced pork and boiled in an earthenware pot. Then green spinach and bean vermicelli, white and semitransparent, are added before they are served piping hot. This pot of egg dumplings, which looks good and tastes good, alone will give a touch of festive mood at the dinner table. There are, of course, pork shreds (*rou si*) fried with bamboo shreds (*sun si*), and so *si si qi qi* which means everything is all right and there is everything everyone wants. There is also a bowl of meat balls signifying happy reunion, a bowl of meat from a pig's head (known as *yuan bao* meat), a bowl of pork and boiled eggs (one for each member of the family, meaning the whole family will survive from generation to generation), and, finally, a bowl of fish, another must. When fish is served, one must not touch its head or tail; this way, one can have "a good start and a good finish." Of course, there is always *tu su* wine for everyone, young and old alike, whether he is a drinker or not. After the wine, faces are crimson and everyone is happy, laughing heartily and cracking jokes.

People of Taiwan call their New Year Eve dinner *wei lu* (sitting round a stove). The whole family will sit at a round table on which a casserole is placed. Those who normally do not drink will have to sip some wine at the dinner. Each and every member of the family is expected to taste all the dishes on the table, for every dish served implies something nice. Thus, fish balls mean reunion, turnip means good omen, chicken (pronounced as *jia* in Taiwanese dialect) means eating it and the whole family (*jia*) will get rich. Some fried foods mean "prosperity." Eating blood clams, pronounced as *pang* (also meaning fat), means one will get rich and gain weight. The vegetables are served whole and eaten whole; they must not be cut into pieces when being prepared in the kitchen and should not be bitten into pieces but swallowed bit by bit. This is a way to wish one's parents long life. When sitting round the casserole, if any one in the family is away from home, there is a vacant seat with clothes placed on it to show that the whole family misses the person.

Night Watch

After dinner, nobody goes to bed. According to *Feng Tu Ji* (*Notes on Local Customs*), "On the New Year Eve, people do not go to bed but sit up to the morning. Guarding the year, it is called." A poem entitled "Guarding the Year" by Su Dongpo reads:

Children refuse to go to bed,
Watching the night together for fun.

Children naturally do not wish to miss the happiest moment

they can have and the grownups just sit and shoot the breeze, with housewives busy steaming, stewing and frying food for the New Year.

That night, every house would be brightly lit, with oil lamps everywhere, both indoors and outdoors, and in the kitchen too. This was supposed to shed a benevolent light on things in all corners that might bring bad luck. In Hangzhou, there was the old custom of climbing up the Wu Hill on the New Year Eve to have a bird's eye view of the whole city — lights in myriads of households glittering and smoke from the burning incense curling upward, now and then firecrackers zooming into the sky and making big noises amidst the sound of drums and gongs. The fireworks would glare in the dark sky, some like red lanterns hanging high overhead, others like flowers in full bloom. That night, housewives would have everything ready for New Year Day sacrifices — colourful paper money, tinfoil papers and fruit, both dried and fresh.

House Cleaning

Cleaning up the house on the New Year Eve is another age-old custom that is still being observed today.

In the past, many poor people in debt had to make themselves scarce on the New Year Eve to get away from their creditors. In Taiwan, on the New Year Eve, there are theatrical performances staged in monasteries known as "show for those in debt." The people in debt go there to see the show and if and when creditors come to look for them to dun, they will be jeered by the audience.

71

Han People's Folk Customs at Other Festivities

Second month, the twelfth day: Baihua Jie (Hundred Flowers Festival). Said to be the flowers' birthday on which girls wear five-coloured ribbons on the head. Flowers planted on that day are supposed to grow in profusion.

Second month, the fifteenth day: Huazhao Jie (Flower Festival). The second month of a year being in the middle of spring, the fifteenth day of the month is called the Flower Day, on which people enjoy the beauty of flowers, go for outings and catch butterflies (which are considered to be flowers that fly.)

Third month, the third day: Emperors and kings of the ancient times offered sacrifices to heaven on that day, while people of the common run went to city outskirts to offer sacrifices to their ancestors.

Fourth month, the eighth day: Yufo Jie (Washing the Buddha Festival). Said to be the birthday of Sakyamuni. In the old days, people brewed sugar water mixed with fragrant medicinal herbs and called it "water for washing the Buddha" and gave it to others as gift; people would also go to a temple and burn incense at the altar and give alms — considered as another way of "washing the Buddha."

Fourth month, the thirteenth day: Said to be the birthday of Lü Dongbin, one of the eight immortals worshipped by Taoist priests. In the past, people went to the Temple of Lü the

Forerunner that day to burn incense and for divination.

Fourth month, the fifteenth day: Said to be the birthday of the Tang Dynasty princess Wen Cheng, who married a Tibetan king and was marked by people in Tibet.

Fifth month, the thirteenth day: Said to be the birthday of Guan Yu, a general of the State of Shu in the period of the Three Kingdoms. Also said to be the day Guan Yu sharpened his sword. It almost always turns out to be rainy day because, so people say, sharpening a sword needs water.

Sixth month, the first day: People of north China marked this day as "New Year in the middle of the year," formerly a day to fight against pestilence.

Sixth month, the thirteenth day: Observed in the south as the birthday of Lu Ban, an ancient architect, who would be offered sacrifices on that day by carpenters and bricklayers.

Sixth month, the fifteenth day: In the north, it is said to be the birthday of the Sun God. People would get up early to ascend a height to greet the rising sun and pray for a bright future.

Folk Customs of the Minority Peoples at Their Main Traditional Festivities

1. Tibetan New Year

The Tibetan people long ago had their own astronomical calendar. Having settled down in Tibet in A.D. 641, Princess Wen Cheng of the Tang Dynasty played a part in promoting cultural exchange between the Han and Tibetan peoples, in the course of which the Tibetan calendar was further improved and developed. The Tibetan calendar was officially adopted in 1027, or the fifth year of the reign of Tian Sheng under the Song Emperor Ren Zong. That year, according to the Chinese lunar calendar, was the year of Ding Mao. Thus, this very year was made the first year on the Tibetan calendar in its first sixty-year cycle. By now, according to the Tibetan calendar, the Tibetans are living in the sixteenth cycle.

The Tibetan calendar is a combination of the solar and lunar calendars. A year is divided into 12 months with 30 days for a big month and 29 days for a small month. Every two years and a half to three years, there is a leap month for readjusting the interrelationship between months and seasons. Generally speaking, after the Han people have celebrated their Spring Festival, the Tibetans are about to celebrate their own New Year.

The Tibetan New Year is the most important festival for Tibetans. People in different parts of Tibet do not mark the New Year Day on the same day: In Lhasa, the New Year Day falls on the first day of the first month on the Tibetan calendar; in places south of the Nyangqu-River, it falls on the first day of the twelfth month; in some places round Qamdo, it is the first day of the eleventh month.

The Tibetans in different parts of the region celebrate their New Year in different ways. In Lhasa, on the New Year Day, every family will spread lime on their doorsteps, drawing up designs symbolizing good luck. Everyone will put on his or her holiday best. Men appear in a loose woollen garment with the right arm ·slipped out of the sleeve to show the white undergarment or a woollen sweater inside, a broad silk sash round the waist, a four-flap hat of brocade knit with golden and silvery threads and long boots. Women wear even more colourful and fancy dresses: the material used is even better than the men's. The garment from the collar down is opened on a slant to show the silk blouse inside. She has her hair piled up, fixed by red and green woollen threads, and topped by a headgear. She will wear earrings, of course. Most women wear leather shoes except a few elderly women who will probably wear red felt shoes.

On the New Year Day, people generally do not go out to call on friends or relatives but stay home to celebrate the occasion with their own people. After having washed faces and brushed teeth, the first thing the younger people do is salute the elderly people, especially paying respects to their grandmother who is in charge of household affairs. Then, the housewife, representing the whole family, will extend New Year greetings to the neighbours. For a full day the whole family drinks *qingke* wine (made from highland barley) and eats Tibetan food, like dried meat, sausage, mutton stewed with turnip and cake made of sugar, butter and milk residue. They go on eating from noon to night and many of them are dead drunk by the afternoon.

On the second day, people go out to visit other families, exchanging greetings. Wine is offered by hosts and everywhere there is laughter and dance music. The streets are crowded; theatrical companies stage roadside shows to entertain the public.

In pastural areas, the New Year celebrations last seven days, beginning from the first day of the month. On the twenty-ninth of the previous month, every family begins house-cleaning to dispose of sewage and rubbish by throwing them away westward before sunset. In so doing they expect the sun to get rid of evil things and the sunlight to destroy all foul things. On the New Year Eve, people begin making butter and milk cakes, preparing meat that will be eaten by hand, sausages, and milk, fresh and sour. On the New Year Day the housewife must get up early to fetch water home. Anyone who carries water back first is considered the one who will live in happiness. Joss sticks are planted at the place of water supply and the first cask of clear water carried back is to be mixed with a little milk for the whole family to wash their faces and for the domestic animals to drink their fill. Then the whole family sits down to eat. Before eating anything the family must first eat some dry flour of *qingke* barley to remind themselves that they are persons who live on *zamba* (Tibetan people's staple food made of *qingke* barley). In fact, the Tibetans like to describe themselves as people with dark hair living on *zamba*. Food for the New Year Day is plentiful: congee, meat broth, steamed buns, buns with stuffings, beef and mutton. Between the first and third day of the New Year, people as a rule do not leave the village in which they live; in some places, they ask one neighbouring family after another to dinner; in other places only relatives and friends are

Tibetan New Year.

invited. Between the fourth and seventh day, they may go anywhere they wish and call on relatives. During the New Year, girls and married women appear in groups and "snatch" food from men, who must not protest. In the evening, they get together to eat, to sing and play.

In some places, celebrations begin on the New Year Eve. That day there will be a grand meeting at which a sorcerers' dance is performed. People in colourful dresses and wearing weird masks sing aloud and dance like mad to the accompaniment of drums, *suona* (horn) and the conch. The dance, they hope, will exorcise evil spirits and win God's blessings. On the New Year Day, women go and carry home "water of good luck." Every family makes cake with butter and *qingke* barley flour; a few bundles of wheat ear and *qingke* dyed in colour are planted on the cake to celebrate in advance a bumper harvest. People also exchange greetings and *hata*. *Hata* is a specially made long silk scarf of different colours, mostly white, semi-transparent and extremely light. To offer someone a *hata* means offering him a pure, friendly heart. To offer *hata*, one must present it with both hands as a sign of respect and say something nice. After the ceremony all get together to sing and dance. Tibetans are good singers and excellent dancers. The songs are melodious and the words are in rhyme. Singing is accompanied by dancing — solo, pas de deux or group. Some dances are limited either to movements of the upper body, the waist and the arms or to movements of the lower body, the legs and the feet; the tap dance is a very peculiar one. Dance music, very melodious, and the instruments used are patterned after those in the interior. The instruments for lama music, however, include mainly drums with long sticks and long bugles, producing the sound of nature and the call of the birds and beasts, which can be heard several kilometres away, giving an additional touch to the festive mood.

There are many gardens, called *lingka*, in the suburbs of

Tibetan cities and townships. During the New Year, people picnic in them. Young people often get together in *lingka* to look for the one he or she likes.

In some places, on the second day of the Tibetan New Year, girls seventeen years of age will have their hair formally dressed. A Tibetan girl has 3 pigtails at the age of 13 or 14, 5 at 15 or 16, and when she is 17, she will have dozens of them. Hairdressing is a ceremonial occasion. The parents will give their daughter a new beautiful dress and headgear and ask a woman skilled in hairdressing to help her.

Other recreations during the New Year holiday include horse racing, archery contests and yak race contests.

2. Tibetan Bathing Festival

Bathing Festival is another traditional festivity of the Tibetan people. It takes place every year in late summer and early autumn, from the day when the Wild Rat Star becomes visible in the district of Lhasa to the day it is out of sight — a seven-day event.

This festival is seven to eight hundred years old. One year in autumn, it is said, a serious epidemic visited Tibet, threatening the life of people and their animals. People hurried to offer sacrifices to heaven and burn incense to ask for the blessing of heaven. Guan Yin, the Goddess of Mercy, or Avalokitesvara, thus sent seven fairy maids down and poured seven bottles of holy water from the jade vase of the Goddess into rivers, lakes and ponds in Tibet. That night everyone dreamed of a girl, sallow and emaciated, her body covered all over with ulcers, jumping into a river for a bath and coming out with a sound body and a lovely feature. Sick people after waking up flocked to have a dip in a river and they were all cured.

Although this story sounds a bit fantastic, taking baths in a

Tibetan Bathing Festival.

river at that season of the year is, in reality, certainly good for one's health. Tibet is a highland where winter is long and summer short; in spring immediately after the thawing of ice and snow the river water is bitingly cold, not fit for a bath; in summer, torrents of water rush down from mountains with both sand and mud, which makes the river water muddy and cold, also not fit for a bath. Only in early autumn, when the river water is clear and clean and water temperature is just right, is it the right season for bathing outdoors. It is said that water in early autumn is sweet, cool, soft, light, clear, ordourless and that it does not harm one's throat or stomach when one drinks it; on the contrary, it prevents certain diseases and cures some other diseases and has the function of preventing colds.

At the time of the Bathing Festival, all over the Tibetan Plateau, the "roof of the world," people of all ages and both sexes appear in groups to bathe in rivers, lakes and ponds, to swim and wash their clothing. By the Lhasa River, everyday thousands of people come to celebrate, young people playing in water, women taking a bath and washing laundry at the riverside, children romping at the beach. On the embankment several kilometres long, washed clothes and sheets are everywhere. Seen from a distance, they look like many multi-coloured ribbons. People after bathing sit in tents under trees drinking *qingke* wine and buttered tea in a jovial, festive mood.

3. Dong People's Firecracker Day

The annual Firecracker Day is the most important festival marked by the Dong people for more than a hundred years. In the early days under the reign of Guangxu of the Qing Dynasty, Fulo in Sanjiang County, Guangxi, was already an entrepot of timber and a commercial centre. Merchants in the locality, with a view to promoting business, sponsored a firecracker exhibition on the third day of the third lunar month to attract customers. Winners at the exhibition were not only honoured but given material awards such as wine, meat and eggs. Year after year, the event has developed into a tradition — the Firecracker Day.

The date of the festivity varies from place to place. Take the Sanjiang Dong Autonomous County in northern Guangxi for instance. It falls on the third day of the first month in Chengyang, on the second day of the second month in Meiling, on the third day of the third month in Fulo and on the twenty-sixth day of the tenth month in Linxi. One or two days before the festivity, people living in the locality where the exhibition is to be held will receive their relatives and friends from other places and lodge them as guests to mark the occasion together.

Early in the morning of the festivity, all villages and stockades are jubilant. There are people everywhere, girls in new embroidered dresses wearing silver ornaments and young men in black jackets and long white trousers with puttees. The site of assembly is decorated with colourful pennants and on a makeshift stage musicians play the *suona*, the drums and the gongs. Professional art performers and amateur singers put on local shows the Dong people fancy. There are stalls selling food and other things. People of other nationalities living in the vicinity come to join them.

The festival activity begins with the setting off of three firecrackers. They are iron tubes containing gunpowder, each with a small iron ring wrapped in red and green threads. When the explosion cracks, the iron ring zooms into the sky, winning the applause of the onlookers. As soon as it drops on the ground, tense and alert young men, anxious to recover the ring, rush for it like gushing torrents from a lifted dam. The crowd also runs along with the young people, now to the east, now to the west. Sometimes, the ring, the symbol of happiness and good luck, happens to drop into a river, so the young men, too,

Dong people's Firecracker Day.

jump into it and continue the scramble. The one who finally gets hold of the ring has to outwit his rivals who try to encircle him. He has to throw off his pursuers, bypass their interceptions, and reach the terminal to become the winner. Winners are respected and receive awards from elderly people.

The event is immediately followed by various recreational and sports activities. The reed-pipe bands of various villages and stockades will also enter a contest, blowing huge pipes and various kinds of exquisitely made mini pipes. Young people will engage in shooting contests. Others either sing and dance, or engage in dialogue singing to show affection for each other. The middle-aged and the old drink wine, listen to opera singing, watch birdfighting or play chess. There is also a fair at the festival.

By night, all Dong villages in the mountains are brightly lit. Merry-making includes watching a local opera or seeing a movie. From the two-storeyed wooden buildings come the sweet voices of people singing Dong folk songs, accompanied by the *pipa* (a stringed instrument) and the *lu* flute music.

4. Dai People's Water Splashing Festival

In Xishuangbanna, Yunnan, the Dai people's New Year falls in the period between the twenty-fourth and twenty-sixth day of the sixth month on the Dai calendar, about a fortnight after the Han people's Qing Ming Festival.

The festival has a beautiful, legendary background. Long, long ago, there lived a fierce, brutal Demon King in Xishuangbanna, who had tremendous magic power that made many people suffer. He had seven wives and they all hated him. The seventh wife was pretty, young and clever. One day she said to her husband: "O, my lord, how powerful and able you are. I wish you live on forever." The Demon King was pleased to hear that and confided to her his secret: "But I too am vulnerable. Suppose someone cut into my neck with my own hair, I'll be finished." In that evening, when he was fast asleep, his seventh wife plucked a hair of his and used it to cut into his neck, and, sure enough, his big head fell off and dropped on the floor. But, alas! Wherever the head rolled, disaster followed. It rolled on the ground and the ground was on fire; it rolled into a river and the river water boiled and fish in it died; when it was buried underground, the whole place stank. So she had no alternative but keeping the head in her arms in order that it might not bring people havoc. After some time, she was exhausted and looked haggard. So the six others took over one by one in turn. When at rest, they splashed water on their body to wash away the bloodstains. In memory of the seven brave women who were ready to suffer themselves so that others would not, water is splashed on them once a year — one day in heaven, it is said, means a year on earth.

The first day of the festival is the day to send off the old and bring in the new. Usually, people do not splash water on that day, but have dragon boat regattas on the Lancang River. In remote antiquity, according to a legend, there was in Xishuangbanna a feudal lord hated by everyone. One day he insisted on having a boat race with a poor young man and declared: "If you lose, I'll chop your head off to feed the fish in the river." Now the feudal lord had a big boat capable of carrying a thousand catties of cargo while the poor young man had only a small one. The latter nevertheless accepted the challenge. His dauntlessness moved the Dragon King and the God. On the day of the race, the Dragon King metamorphosed itself into a big ship for the young man to sail in and the God too blew up a gale for the sail to catch. In an instant, there was a storm over the Lancang River which capsized the feudal lord's boat and drowned him. To do honour to the memory of that brave young man, people have a dragon boat regatta on the first day of the Water Splashing Festival.

Each village is a contestant in the regatta. A dragon boat has upturned stem and stern and its body is colourfully painted. At the bow is a carved wooden dragon's head and at the stern a tail. Young people taking part in rowing have on red turbans and look very smart and athletic. All boats push hard to forge ahead after the starter's order. On the boats the oarsman chant in unison while onlookers on both banks of the river repeatedly cheer. The dragon boats speed on like darting arrows or like sea serpents riding on waves. When the winners come to land they are given a big banner to mark their victory, together with rice wine and sweets. Afterwards, in the midst of music, they join other young people at the river bank in dancing.

Water splashing takes place on the second day. There are two ways of splashing water. The so-called moderate one is applied to elderly people only. When splashed, the recipient must not walk away. The one who splashes, muttering some words of a good wish, dips an olive branch into a basin of clear water and lets off a few drops on an elderly person's head, or ladles up a spoonful of clear water, still muttering a good wish, and pulls open the elderly person's collar to pour water down along his spine. The so-called radical one is to throw basinfuls of water onto anyone, on his or her face and on his or her whole body. Water splashing is the Dai people's ritual of bestowing blessings on others. The more water splashed means the greater blessings and the more happiness for the recipient. In April 1961, the late Premier Zhou Enlai, dressed in a Dai costume of silvery gray and with a red turban, joined the Dai people in celebrating their Water Splasing Festival.

By night, every village has social gatherings for singing and dancing. Beating *xiangjiaogu* (a drum on a pedestal, shaped like an elephant's leg), to the accompaniment of the bamboo flute, *lu sheng* (a wind-pipe instrument) and gongs of the local type, people dance the native peacock dance. The region inhabited by the Dai people teems with peacocks and is known as the land of peacocks. People there look on the peacock as the symbol of good luck and dance the native peacock dance to extend good wishes to everyone. The movements in this dance are imitations of the movements of a peacock and the dancer dresses up as a peacock. It is a dance for a group of people who, slightly tipsy, often sing as they dance. Both the singing and the dance steps are impromptu, lively and with some sense of humour so that onlookers often burst into laughter. It is a typical native dance. And the singers, known locally as *zan ha*, sing of the legends of the festival. The gathering sometimes lasts until midnight.

The third day of the festival is described by the Dais as "the day of days," meaning the New Year Day. Celebrations on that day come to a climax when people begin to set off *gao sheng* (going up high, or firecrackers), and *diu bao* (throwing pouches).

Gao sheng is a kind of home-made rocket, a bamboo tube stuffed with gunpowder. Light the fuse and the bamboo tube, propelled by the momentum of the gunpowder in combustion, zooms skyward whistling. Inside the biggest *gao sheng* are placed by custom five little souvenirs which go up into the sky with it. When they fall down on the ground, people rush to pick them up because to get one of them means good luck.

Diu bao is the most lively, most interesting event in the Water Splashing Festival celebrations; it is also an occasion for young men and women to look for someone to love or to show affection for someone. The *bao* is a pouch triangular in shape, made of cloth with cotton seeds inside, and its hems are laced with colourful tassels. The game begins with boys and girls standing in two rows face to face throwing sacks to each other. Whoever fails to catch it will offer the other party flowers by way of an apology. As the game goes on, some boys or girls may fall for each other and they will step forward in pairs and come closer to each other. When a girl has chosen the boy she likes,

Dai people's Water Splashing Festival.

she will suddenly snatch the sword he bears, or his headgear or his other belongings and run back home to have dinner ready for the boy she loves.

5. Bai People's Third Month Fair

This is a big festival and fair for the Bai people, taking place between the fifteenth and twentieth of the third month at the foot of Diancang Hill to the west of Dali City, Yunnan Province. At first, it was more or less a kind of religious rite, but gradually it has developed into a grand trading affair.

The festivity was called the Guanyin Day in ancient times (Guanyin is also known as the Goddess of Mercy). It became a fair in the Tang Dynasty under the reign of Yong Hui (A.D. 650-655) about 1,300 years ago. According to a Buddhist anecdote, long, long ago, there was a Raksasa Demon near Lake Erhai, who pecked out the eyeballs of over thirty people a day. The Goddess of Mercy, who could not bear to see the Bai people suffer, overpowered the demon with her supernatural magic and tied him on a column in a palace hall. Out of gratitude, the Bai people pitched up canopies to chant scriptures on the fifteenth of the third month, the day Guanyin descended on the mundane world. By and by, it became a traditional festivity of the Bai people.

Another anecdote tells of a fisherman named Ah Shan, who lived by Lake Erhai. One day he went out to the lake to fish but got no catch in his dragnet. Disappointed, he sang and played his fiddle in a melancholy way, which won the sympathy of the third princess Ah Xiang of the Dragon King of Lake Erhai. She came on the boat, helped him trawl and they had a good haul. When working with Ah Shan, Ah Xiang fell in love with him. He brought her home, and they lived happily as man and wife. Now the fifteenth of the third month was the day for the annual fair in the moon, to be attended by deities from everywhere. Ah Xiang transformed herself into a golden dragon and carried Ah Shan on her back to go to the fair together. They saw pearls, gems, miraculous medicinal herbs at the moon fair but no farm implements or fish nets. When they returned to the village they told the villagers what they saw at the moon fair and they all agreed to have a fair of their own. Thus, every year on that day, people hold a fair at the foot of Diancang Hill.

Whatever the mythological background of the festival may be, the annual Third Month Fair today has become an important festival of the Bai people, an occasion for commercial and cultural exchange between people of different nationalities. People of many nationalities come to the fair — Yis, Tibetans, Lisus, Naxis, Nus, Huis and Hans.

The Third Month Fair in Dali is a busy affair. A forest of coloured streamers fly on the street with tents displaying all sorts of merchandise. People in their holiday best swarm into the place to look for things they want and sell their own native products at the fair. What attracts the customers most at the fair are the counters selling special products for minority peoples: silk threads for Bai women to sew collars on their garments, bracelets, earrings, pearl necklaces and waist chains for Bai girls, felt hats and butter pots for Tibetans, lace and ribbons for the Naxis and Yis.

The most eye-catching merchandise at the fair, however, are marble artifacts of world fame: table tops, flower pots, cups, dishes, all unique in design and of excellent craftsmanship. These products made by the Bai people fully demonstrate their wisdom. And the fine, beautiful embroidered articles — head scarves with many decorative lines on them, embroidered cloth shoes in bright red or green, bags embroidered with dragons and phoenixes, aprons with love birds on water — are equally lovely. Taking many hours to make, scarves are often given by a Bai girl to her sweetheart as an engagement souvenir.

Bai people's Third Month Fair Legend.

For sale at the Third Month Fair are also many famous special and native products, such as locally grown fungus, preserved sweets, mushrooms, black fungus, home-made paper, furniture and so on. Fish in an earthware pot, a speciality of Dali, is cooked with over a dozen ingredients and condiments — highly nourishing and really tasty. Horses bred in Dali are of choice strain; the battle steed the famous general Yue Fei of the Southern Song Dynasty had was said to have come from Dali.

In streets near the Third Month Fair are open-air movies, stage shows and ball games. During the festival people take part in horse racing, archery contests and dancing parties.

6. Yao People's Danu Festival

Danu Festival, or the Woman Ancestor's Day, or the Day of the King Pan Gu, or the Yao's Year, is the most important traditional festivity of the Yao people living in Guangxi and other places. It falls on the twenty-ninth day of the fifth lunar month. Danu in the Yao language means never forget the past. A grand occasion it is, taking place but once every three to five years, and, in some places, once only in every twelve years, depending on the traditional customs of the locality concerned and on how good the hearvest is and how well men and their animals fare.

Of the many touching stories about the festival, here is a fairly well-told one: In remote antiquity, Miluotuo Goddess, the Yao's ancestor, told her three daughters to go to the mundane world and live on their own. The next morning, her eldest daughter got up early, carrying a plough with her to plough the land on a plain. She had many children and children's children, who were later known as the Han people. Her second daughter rose and carried books to study somewhere. Her offspring were known as the Zhuang people, who are well versed in the art of playing the lute, and in chess, in calligraphy, painting and singing. The third daughter did not get up until late in the morning. When she saw there was nothing left for her, she cried. So Miluotuo gave her all the rice left and told her to reclaim land in a mountain. But when the rice plants began to sprout, wild cats came for them; when they began to grow, deer came to nibble at them; and when the crops ripened, birds came to peck at them. She complained to her mother of the trouble, crying, and mamma gave the youngest daughter a copper drum she had kept for many years. The youngest daughter brought it to the mountain and beat it when she had nothing to do and felt bored. She beat the drum also to drive away birds and animals coming to devastate her crops. In the end, there was a bountiful harvest and she settled down in the mountain and lived there happily. Her descendants were known as the Yao people. To honour the memory of their ancestor, the Yaos made the twenty-ninth of the fifth month, Miluotuo's birthday, the Danu Festival.

On the eve of the festival, the Yaos will clean their houses and prepare all kinds of food and wine. On the festive day, they all wear clothes in bright colours and go to a designated place carrying with them wine and food. There, people pool their food and eat together.

During the festival, there are all kinds of entertainment: dialogue singing, playing the *suona*, playing hide-and-seek, displaying martial arts (*wu shu*), and the most interesting events: the copper drum dance and sending off rockets.

Copper drum is a kind of percussion instrument popular in some parts of Guangxi, Guangdong, Yunnan and Guizhou inhabited by minority peoples. All made of copper, the drumhead is about 50 cm in diameter and the cylinder is about 30 cm in height. The cylinder, hollow and without a bottom, has two brass ears at both sides. Both the drumhead and the

Yao people's Danu Festival.

body are decorated with fine-carved patterns. Copper drum dance is a folk dance popular among the Yao people and also an item for contest during the festival. The drummers, three in a group, two men and one woman, give performances in turn. One of the man performers beats the drum and dances according to the rhythm of the beat; the other one beats a parchment drum in accompaniment. Some parchment drummers display their excellent skill by beating the drum now sidewise and now to the back of their body and beating it at an increasingly fast tempo. The woman performer holds two rain caps to fan the drummers. The act of fanning itself is a dancing movement, so she does her fanning while dancing. When the one who fans and the one who is being fanned move gracefully in coordination, the audience will warmly applaud. After the contest, people drink toasts to the best drummers.

Sending off rockets takes place in an atmosphere of great excitement. During the contest, people place several rockets on the ground for the contestants, one man and one woman, to light. He or she who succeeds in sending off more rockets into the sky is the winner, to be hailed and saluted, lifted up and thrown into the air.

Today at a Danu Festival, apart from these traditional activities, cultural troupes come to give performances for the Yao people while people of other nationalities also come to extend their congratulations.

7. Yi People's Torch Festival

Beginning from the twenty-fourth of the sixth lunar month, the Yi people have a three-day holiday — the Torch Festival, a festival to express one's sentiments through the medium of fire!

A long time ago, there was a well-known, invincible wrestler named Eqilaba. When the God in heaven heard about him, a good wrestler was sent down to fight him, but was killed in the fight. The God was upset and got angry, sending swarms of "heavenly insects" down to destroy the crops and wreak havoc in the mundane world. Eqilaba and his country folks went to the mountains to fell bamboo, made torches, and lighted the torches to kill the "heavenly insects," finally bringing about a good harvest. To commemorate man's victory over the insects, they repeated the torch ritual every year at the end of the sixth month, along with wrestling, singing and dancing. As time went on, it developed into the Torch Festival of today. Another story about the festival dates back to the Tang Dynasty, when the Yunnan region was divided up and controlled by six tribal chieftains. The most powerful of the six was Meng She, who wanted to annex the domains under the other five tribes. So he constructed a pine torch tower and invited the five other chieftains to come to attend a feast and offer sacrifices to their forebears. The wife of chieftain Deng Shan was suspicious of Meng She's intention and suggested that her husband should not go. Deng, overawed by the power of Meng She, decided to go anyway. So his wife put a metal bracelet on her husband's arm as a precautionary measure. Sure enough, Deng and four other chieftains were burnt alive on the tower. The wives of the chieftains were then notified to go and collect their husbands' remains, which were, however, all charred and could not be identified, with the exception of Deng's, thanks to that metal bracelet he wore. Deng's remains were brought back and interred. Meng She, finding her a very beautiful and intelligent woman, proposed to take her as a concubine but was turned down by the widow of Deng Shan. Upon her return to her own domain, she told the officers and men of the tribal army about what had really happened at the pine torch tower and Meng She's underhanded scheme. When Meng She sent troops to besiege Deng's city, Deng's wife led her husband's troops in

Yi people's Torch Festival.

resisting the invaders. Water and food ran out after the city was beleaguered for three months. Many soldiers were starved to death, so was Deng's wife. To honour the memory of this wise, faithful heroine, the Yi people every year on the twenty-fourth of the sixth month mark the Torch Festival. It was said when Deng's wife was trying to recover her husband's remains, her ten fingers, bruised and cut in the digging, were stained with blood. This is why to this day at the time of the festival, the Yi women still polish their fingernails red with garden balsam juice.

In the early morning of the festival, people begin to dress up. A man will put on an embroidered short jacket with the collar opened slantwise at the right, a pair of loose, baggy trousers, keeping a lock of hair on the top known as *tian sa*. He will wear a red or yellow pearl on his right ear and a blue or black turban with a long "hero's knot" tied near the forehead. A woman will wear an upper garment embroidered and trimmed with lace, and a multifold skirt in variegated colours. She wears earrings, a silver pin with floral designs on the collar, a cloth or a scarf on the head. Both man and woman wear a blanket-like shawl. In daytime the main activities are wrestling, bullfighting, archery contests and horse racing. People drink wine through the celebrations.

The night of the Torch Festival is enchanting. People light up torches and assemble on the village outskirts. Hundreds and thousands of torches are seen moving along paths in the fields like writhing dragons, with the smaller ones wriggling around a big one like myriads of stars round the moon. And the most exciting and interesting scene is that of "splashing fire." People hold torches in their left hands and their pockets or bags are filled with inflammable powder mixed with resin. When someone comes from the opposite direction, they just spread a handful of powder on the torch. And, lo! dazzling flames immediately flash near the one approaching. By then those who did the trick have gone. So the one being "splashed" would hold high his own torch to chase after them and pay them back in their own coin.

This is the climax of the night and after that, young men and women sing and dance around the burning torches. Boys play bamboo flutes, moon-shaped guitars or big three-stringed instruments. Girls dance the moon dance. Everybody is in such high spirits that dancing may go on and on throughout the night until dawn. This is also the occasion for young people to look for a life partner through dialogue singing.

8. Miao People's Catching-the-Autumn Day

Every year on the day of the Beginning of Autumn (Li Qiu), the Miao people in western Hunan observe their traditional Catching-the-Autumn Day.

Catching the autumn (*qiu*) is actually derived from the term catching the swing (*qiu qian*). Once upon a time, says a story, there lived a handsome young man of the Miao nationality named Baguidare. He was not only brave and intelligent but also a man of integrity, always ready to help others. Liked by his people, he was, as the most eligible bachelor, pestered by match-makers. Girls in the ninety-nine villages were secretly in love with him but none of them could win his heart. He wanted to find a girl who was clever, beautiful and kind-hearted.

One good autumn day when he was hunting in a mountain, he saw an eagle with something in its talons flying overhead. He shot it down with an arrow and found that it was a beautiful embroidered shoe that the eagle had seized. Baguidare, feeling that the girl who did such wonderful embroidery work must be very clever and beautiful, decided to look for the girl who made and wore that shoe.

So he built a swing that could seat a number of people and invited all the girls in the neighbourhood to come and have a swing. When they came he checked their shoes with the one he had and finally found his "Cinderella." They got married soon. And the swing instrumental in helping Baguidare find a wife has today become a thing for recreation.

In those days, agricultural production in western Hunan and Songtao district in Guizhou was yet to be developed. Before the autumn harvest people had to go hunting in the mountains to offset the food shortage. When they came back with their game, it was harvest time. Villagers would erect swings invented by Baguidare on the day of Li Qiu and assemble at mountain slopes or at densely populated villages to welcome the hunters home and celebrate the good harvest after a year's hard work. At sites where the swings were, people used sticks made of animal bone to beat the drums stretched with animal hide to amuse themselves. Thus, catching the swing (*qiu qian*) became catching the autumn (*Qiu*), a custom that has been passed down to the present.

On that day, surrounded by a jubilant crowd, newly erected swings seating eight or twelve people start to revolve. There is a rule that whoever wishes to have a swing must be good at singing and when the fast-moving swing suddenly comes to a halt, the one who is on the top is required to sing solo. Those who know how to manoeuvre always take advantage of the inertia of the swing by setting their feet on the beam of the swing and letting themselves slip down to a lower position. Of course, there are always girls and boys who will rather stay at the top and merrily sing to win people's applause and the admiration of the opposite sex.

"Coloured lions," "coloured dragons," ball games and song and dance too are often attractions at the festival. People also find things to buy at stalls set up by pedlars during the festival.

Near the conclusion of the festival, according to a Miao

custom, two prestigious persons will be disguised as "The Old Man Autumn" wishing people a good harvest and a happy autumn.

9. Mongolian People's Nadam Fair

Weather in Inner Mongolia in the seventh lunar month is glorious; the sky looks high and the air is crisp. There, forage grass grows in profusion and cattle and sheep are fat and in good form. There are also plenty of dairy products. It is the best season in the year and time for Nadam, the traditional festival marked by the Mongolians.

Nadam is the Mongolian word for recreation. The Mongolians are a militant people fond of wrestling, horse racing and archery. Nadam is a Mongolian term derived from these three events, which, about two thousand years ago, were already a means of recreation and a way for the nomads in the north to practise martial arts.

In the Liao Dynasty, these sports activities gained popularity among the masses and were made the main events of Nadam.

By the Kin Dynasty, it had become a rule that winners of the three events would be given monetary awards. When the socio-economy and culture of the country flourished under Genghis Khan, who brought all Mongolian tribes under his unified rule and founded the Mongolian Khanate in 1206, Nadam sports meet became a commonplace at such ceremonial occasions as saluting the colours, assigning an army general to a specific military mission, or celebrating military feats. In historical records of the Yuan Dynasty and those at a later date, in the 15th century, there appeared the term "men's three events." In the Qing Dynasty, Nadam sports meets took place at practically every official ceremony, for instance, at a royal banquet, at a meeting of the local administrations (leagues and banners), at a rite offering sacrifices to a boundary mark, on the occasion

Mongolian people's Nadam Fair.

of the promotion of officials or at the ceremony marking the "Immortal Living Buddha's" accession to the top of the hierarchy.

Historically, Nadam had been under the influence of lamaism, especially when it took place at fairs in lamaseries, or at the ritual to offer sacrifices to stone objects used as landmarks, and was associated with religious preaching. Nadam today, while its traditional national form is being kept intact, has developed into something new, something with specific national features, something to the liking of the Mongolian people.

The Nadam sports meet is a joyful one. The Mongolian people have been fond of wrestling since antiquity. It was said that, when a child, Genghis Khan (r. 1206-1227) once wrestled with a cowherd and won in three straight rounds, the cowherd admired him so much that he helped Genghis Khan avenge his father against the enemy. Later when Genghis Khan became the emperor, he decided to make wrestling an important item in examining the physical fitness of his officers and men. The people at large too made wrestling one of men's three events along with horsemanship and archery. Since then, from generation to generation, wrestling has developed into a very popular sport.

A formal wrestling contest is a very ceremonious affair. Participants will have to wear a traditional costume: a sleeveless jacket made of canvas or leather, which is studded with silver or copper nails; below is a tri-colour short skirt, a pair of embroidered breeches and high boots. The wrestlers will first perform a wrestlers' dance and sing a wrestlers' song, which says: "Send over your brave men, your brave men!" According to the rules of the contest, when any part of the body above the knee touches the ground, the match is lost. Every time a wrestler wins a first prize, he gets a strip of multi-coloured cloth pinned on the chest. A man of the most formidable strength, or a banner champion, wins the title *na qin*, meaning the powerful eagle, and is seen as charismatic and highly regarded among the masses.

Horse racing in Mongolia is closely bound up with animal husbandry and the way of life on the grasslands. The race generally covers scores of kilometres. Before it begins, all riders come to position along a line, each wearing a coloured waistband and a coloured turban. The Mongolian way of horse racing is quite peculiar: riders during the race sit straight on horseback and rein in the horse to make it trot at a speed no slower than galloping.

At the beginning of every event, an elderly man holds high a silver bowl filled with fresh milk and a snow-white *hata* and chants something to give the riders his blessings. This eulogy from horseback before the race is peculiar to the Mongolian nation.

Horses are the herdsmen's best pals in their daily life and also their means of production. On the turf, they vie with one another for the first place and the horse which wins the race will receive great publicity and cause its rider to be justly proud. Thus, the eulogy on horse is well turned — words of encouragement before a race and words of congratulations for the winner and words of consolation for the losers.

Nadam is also a fair. There are makeshift department stores, restaurants, art studios, book shops and pharmacists, one·next to the other; together they make up a shopping centre. Holiday-makers, still excited after having taken part in the horse races and other activities, come to buy things they want.

After dusk, the grassland is brightly lit and the sound of the *matouqin* (a stringed Mongolian instrument with a scroll carved like a horse's head) vibrates in the night air.

10. Id Corban

Id corban is an Islamic festival, more widely known as the

grand prayer meeting day. In China there are ten different nationalities whose religious faith is Islam. These peoples are: the Huis, Uygurs, Kazaks, Kirgizs, Tajiks, Tatars, Ozbeks, Dongxiangs, Salars, and Bonans. Corban is also known as the big year celebrations, which are highly ceremonial.

Id in Arabic means festival and *corban* means sacrifice or dedication. The Chinese translation for the two words is *zaisheng jie* (the festival of butchering animals), that is, the day to slaughter animals as an offering. It was said that Ibrahim the Prophet in a dream got a revelation from Allah that he should slaughter his own son Ismail as a token of piety. But at the very moment Ibrahim was brandishing a knife to do so, a special messenger sent by Allah brought him a sheep and told him to slaughter it instead of dedicating his son. Since then, it has become a custom of the Arab people to slaughter animals every year as offerings. After the founding of Islam, the tenth day of the twelfth month on the Islamic calendar was made the Corban Festival. Since there is a difference of eleven days every year between the Gregorian and Islamic calendars, the date of the annual Corban on the Gregorian calendar is not the same.

In China the various nationalities belonging to the Islamic faith consider Corban a red-letter day. On the eve of the festival, families sweep clean their houses and get busy making cakes and other refreshments. On the festive day, Muslims bathe and attend services; the well-to-do families each butcher a sheep, while some even butcher a cow or a camel for their guests or to give away the meat to friends and relatives. Some Muslims assemble at a mosque, shaking hands, hugging each other and exchanging greetings. After that, led by the Imam, they chant hymns, say prayers and attend the rite of butchering animals. Others go to see friends or relatives, who will entertain visitors according to the traditional protocol — a sumptuous feast at which they eat cakes, fruit and mutton. This is followed by singing and dancing, which sometimes lasts till midnight.

Some minority peoples have their own distinctive way of celebrating the festival according to their own customs.

The Tajiks, for instance, will sweep clean their houses and spread some wheat flour on the wall. Tajik women will spread flour on the left shoulder of their men and guests to wish them good health. In early morning, people enter their houses following a child, who leads a sheep and goes in first. Then they may leave home and pay visits to other families. This, it is said, will ensure that both people and livestock thrive and that there will be a good harvest next year.

The Kazaks, who are good singers and dancers, besides singing and dancing, eat good food and drink wine that day, celebrating the festival with such activities as snatching-the-sheep contests and girl-chasing-after-boy games.

Snatching the sheep is a sport on horseback. A sheep, with its four feet bound, is placed where riders can swoop by and snatch at it. Teams of riders represent villages, and he who succeeds in snatching it up first and sending it back to his village is the winner.

Girls chasing after boys is another game on horseback; it is the young Kazaks' way of courting each other. It begins with a boy and a girl riding on galloping horses. On the way, the boy may flirt with the girl, who may try to evade without answering his questions, but she must never turn him down. A young man who likes the girl may try and block her by means of his excellent horsemanship to prevent her from reaching a preset point. Once they have reached it, the boy, on the way back, rides in front of the girl, who will chase after him and when she has caught up with him, may lash him with a whip and the boy must not fight back. This results in an interesting scene: the boy trying to run away and the girl spurring her horse on to chase after him. If she likes him, she probably will raise her whip high but lash him very lightly, not wishing to hurt him. But if that girl does not feel loving towards the boy it is almost certain that he will get some solid whacks.

Girls chasing after boys at the Id Corban Festival.

Snatching the sheep at the Id Corban Festival.

Snatching the sheep and girls chasing after boys are two popular events at Corban, at Lesser Bairam, or at a wedding. Kazak herdsmen will without fail come to watch on fine horses and bring fruit, wine and other food. People laugh, applaud and cheer every time some one has snatched the sheep or when a girl has caught up with a boy.

11. Lesser Bairam

This is one of the grand festivities of the Islamic world, the end of the Ramadan. In China, minority peoples of the Islamic faith observe rites and make celebrations to mark the occasion. This festival falls annually on the first day of the tenth month on the Islamic calendar. In Xinjiang, it is also known as Ruzi Festival. *Ruzi* is the Persian word for fasting. In other places like Ningxia, it is known as Id Festival. *Id-el-fitr* is the Arabic word for coming back. The Koran explicitly stipulates every adult Muslim must undergo a month's fasting every year.

It takes place in the ninth month on the Islamic calendar. It is said that the Koran was brought to the mundane world by Mohammed the Prophet in the month of fasting, which is a main religious duty of the Muslims. During this period, they have their pre-fast meal before sunrise, eating and drinking to their fill. But between sunrise and sunset, they must neither drink nor eat and those who smoke must quit smoking temporarily. During the month they are required to suppress all kinds of desires and evil ideas, and there will be no sex — all for the purpose of showing their devotion to Allah. They must eat only when there is no sunlight — in the night. To protect the health of lying-in women, women discharging menses, children, the aged, the sick and travellers, these people need not fast. But they, too, must restrain themselves as much as possible in eating and drinking and never eat or drink in public. Those who have been sick will have to fast, as soon as they have recovered, for as many days they have missed; so will the travellers as soon as they have reached their destination. Anyone who fails to fast without a good reason will have to fast two months for every day he has missed, or, he may give up some food grain for sixty people to eat (two catties per person) in a day. Throughout the month of fasting, the atmosphere is solemn. However, the end of fasting in the night, people may eat, drink, talk and banter or get together to have a good time with their neighbours; even strangers who happen to pass by may drop in anyone's home and will be warmly received by the host.

At the end of the Ramadan comes the Lesser Bairam, or the Festival of Fast-breaking. In the early morning on the first of the tenth month on the Islamic calendar, Muslims, in their holiday best, assemble at mosques for ablutions and prayer. Celebrations follow. Men usually visit and greet relatives and friends on that day; women in the next few days. In Xinjiang, streets are crowded with people, who, beating small drums like a tambourine and playing the *dongbula* (a plucked stringed instrument), sing and dance on the spot. Even horses are caparisoned and their manes and tails are decorated with pheasant feathers tied up with red silk; both the saddles and harnesses are covered with floral ornaments. Uygur Muslims receive relatives and friends at home, offering them milk tea, almond, dried apricots, raisins, honey and light refreshments. The Kazaks, Kirgizs and Tajiks play the game of snatching the sheep and other sports events on horseback. Muslims in the south will make deep-fried sesame oil dough cake for themselves and their relatives and friends. In other parts of the country Muslims will have get-together on that day. Young people about to get married often choose this day as their nuptial day.

China adopts a policy of respecting the customs of the various nationalities and the freedom of religion. The Lesser

The Islamic Lesser Bairam (Breaking the Fast Day).

Bairam is a holiday in places where minority people of the Islamic faith live in a compact community. The local department of commerce sees to it that Muslims get an additional supply of special food for the festival.

12. Shui People's Duan Festival

Duan Jie in the Shui language means "having a good start." It is the New Year Day of the Shui people in Guizhou Province, much as the Spring Festival is the Han people's lunar New Year Day. According to the Shui calendar, a year begins with the ninth lunar month and the festivity lasts from the late eighth month to the early tenth. When it is a "Hai" day (Hai being the last of the Twelve Earthly Branches, so one out of every twelve days is a Hai day), the Shui people in various places mark the festival in turn according to an established custom. It is a festival to celebrate a good harvest and wish people good luck in the coming year.

There are many stories about the origin of the festival. The more widely told story is about three brothers driven by flood to a place which is now the Sanjiang Shui Autonomous Prefecture in Guizhou. They were pained to see the villages and houses go to rack and ruin in the flood. They all vowed to rebuild the flood-hit areas and vowed to meet again next year that day, the first Hai day in the first month on the Shui calendar. A year later, they met again to tell each other what they had done in the drive for rehabilitation. To pay respects to their forebears, the Shui people made the day a festive day.

On the eve of the festival, all villages are resonant with the sound of brass gongs, the gongs that are rarely struck except on red-letter days. They struck to announce the advent of the New Year. Alerted, every family will start checking to see if everything for the festival is ready. On the morning of the festival, new clothes are put on and many foods are prepared as sacrifices to the forebears. They cook new glutinous rice and make soup with live fish fresh from water. Guests are entertained and people exchange visits, wishing each other better lives every year. During the festival, the Shui people have horse racing, beat drums, play the *lusheng* reedpipe and dance for amusement.

Horse racing usually takes place on a mountain slope near the villages. Such a site is known as the Duan slope or "new year slope." Young participants go to the site with their horses, which are carefully decorated, with bells on the harness, floral balls on the ears and a thick woollen blanket on the back. The racing takes place amid the cheers and applause of the excited spectators.

Beating drums can be a very interesting event, with both copper and parchment drums. The former are golden yellow in colour, with a diameter of 1.5 feet and weighing over 30 kilogrammes; the latter can be a hollowed Paulownia trunk 2.5 feet in length with both the top and bottom stretched with cow hide. The copper drum is beaten in the night of the festival. A family with such a drum will hang it in the middle of a room and amuse themselves by beating it. Young people will then start blowing the *lusheng* and performing copper drum and bull-fighting dances. The drum dance is a bold, exuberant dance to liven things up. The beat of the drum, which begins at a slow tempo, gets faster and faster, and its sound, soft at the beginning, becomes louder and louder. The swift, firm dancing steps are accompanied by the beats of the drums that sound very majestic. The bull-fighting dance is a Shui dance developed at a later date than the drum dance; it is performed usually in years of good harvest. It describes in steps and movements the different stages of farming — seeding, cultivating young plants and harvesting — while artistically interpolating the movements of bull-fighting into the different stages of farming.

13. Zhuang People's March the Third Festival

The third day of the third lunar month is the day for the Zhuang people to sing songs (*ge yu*), the day of *ge po* (song and dance).

Ge yu is the Han term for the Zhuang expression *huan long dong*, which means songs people sing in the fields. In some places, it is called *huan wo gan*, meaning songs sung outside a cave. In the past, the Zhuang people, who seldom built temples, kept their idols in caves, supposed to be holy places, where people must keep quiet and make no noise. So, only after they had left the caves were they free to sing.

"And now Guangxi has become a sea of songs, all passed down personally by the Third Sister." These are words from a folk song in Guangxi; they give the origin of the festival, which is closely connected with the fairy singer Third Sister Liu.

Third Sister Liu was said to be a fisherman's daughter born in Yishan, Guangxi, in the Tang Dynasty. She had loved singing ever since she was a child; when she grew up to become a beautiful girl, she could sing songs impromptu. A wealthy man in the locality named Mo Huairen, drunk with her beauty, hired four singers to engage Third Sister Liu in dialogue singing in the hope that if his men won in the singing contest, they might be able to persuade her to marry Mo. But all four lost the contest. She was then spirited away by Mo's bodyguards. Kidnapped, Third Sister Liu refused to yield, threats and coaxing on the part of Mo notwithstanding. Furious, Mo had her thrown into a river. She was saved from drowning when she was carried downstream to Liuzhou. Presently, she settled down in Yufeng (Fish Peak) Hill and the country folk, on hearing about her, all came to learn singing from her. Later, she married a young hunter and continued teaching people singing. When Mo got wind of this, he schemed to drown her and her husband in a small pool at the foot of

103

Yufeng Hill with the help of some local government officials. In a moonlit starry night, the country folk came to the pool and recovered their corpses. Suddehly in a gust of wind, she and the young hunter were seen riding on a fish singing and drifting in the air before disappearing from the scene. She was believed to have become a deity and ever since the local inhabitants have referred to her as the Fairy Singer. To honour her memory, every year on the third day of the third month, songs are sung for three days and nights, because that day was the death anniversary of Third Sister Liu. Such is the story about the *ge yu*.

Historical records show that this festival has been observed for more than one thousand years. In *Taiping Huanyu Ji* (*Notes on the Peaceful Universe*) written in the Song Dynasty, its author described how "men and women [of the Zhuang nationality] all dress up ... and sing at a gathering." Folk songs of the Zhuang people were especially well developed after the Song and Yuan dynasties. Vocal concerts became very popular: at wedding ceremonies or other felicitous occasions, people liked to sing for merriment and at festivals. During slack seasons in farming, there were regular meetings to sing songs together. Dialogue singing was, in fact, a medium for courtship. By the Qing Dynasty, *ge yu* grew into a meeting of several hundred or even several thousand people singing together.

When a *ge yu* is taking place, young people, in their holiday best, gather at hills, in the open fields, in bamboo groves or on grass slopes for improvised dialogue singing — asking each other questions through singing. The questions asked may involve every field of knowledge, ranging from astronomy, geography, history, social life to productive labour. There were, of course, love songs as well. A group of girls and a group of boys will sing songs to one another within a distance of several metres, asking and answering questions in singing. They make no effort to conceal their feelings and sentiments in the presence

Zhuang people's March the Third Festival.

of the onlookers surrounding them. Often, after a day and a night's dialogue singing, they still are quick in response, full of new ideas expressed in a flow of well turned phrases.

Throwing silk balls is another unique event during the festival. In different colours, these silk balls, used to show affection for someone else and in throwing-and-catching contests, are either round, square or triangular in shape, some being in the shape of a fish or a duck. Their sizes vary. On its upper part is a coloured ribbon and at its lower part dangles a cluster of coloured silk tassels about one foot long. After dialogue singing has continued for some time, the singers begin to throw silk balls. A young man and woman will stand in a field separated by a platform and throw the silk balls to the other side over it. If the one on the other side fails to catch the ball, he or she will have to sing or perform something as a penalty. An unmarried young woman sometimes throws a silk ball stealthily to a man she loves and the man often gives her a handkerchief or a towel in return and through dialogue singing, the young woman is betrothed to the man she loves.

Today, the festivity is large in scale, attended by at least two to three thousand and at most over ten thousand people. Singing in chorus are not only young people but also aged veteran singers, who are duty bound to hand down the famous traditional songs to the younger generation. In the course of the *ge yu,* the Zhuang people have created many colourful folk songs so that this traditional festival of a minority people is always resonant with enchanting melodies.

14. Kazak People's Aken Songfest

Every midsummer, when flowers on the steppes are in full bloom, the Aken Songfest of the Kazak people begins.

Aken is the Kazak word for singer. Long, long ago, so a story goes, there was a pretty girl living on the Altay grassland, who had such a beautiful voice that on hearing it even larks would feel reluctant to fly away. One day, as she was playing her *dongbula* by a river and singing a song of her longing for her lover far away, a tribal chief happened to ride by on a horse. Fascinated by her beauty, he sent a matchmaker to ask for her hand. The girl naturally rejected him but he nevertheless forced her family to contract a marriage between him and the girl. As the wedding day was drawing near, a steed one day appeared and flew away with the grief-stricken girl. That horse was actually her sweetheart who had metamorphosed himself into a beast of burden for this purpose. The girl was reluctant to part with her family and neighbours, so she droppd her *dongbula* from the air and lo! it grew by proliferation to become numerous *dongbulas* falling down for her dear ones on earth. They all joined the departing couple in singing and the grassland was turned into a songfest. Since then, during every midsummer, Kazak herdsmen assemble at the grassland and sing, in memory of that happy couple. Year after year, the Aken Songfest continues.

Participants in the singing session are the best singers from different localities, including veteran artists in their sixties, young men making their debut, girls with young ringing voices. It is a gathering at which every singer vies for the championship.

The Kazaks have the habit of drinking koumiss before the songfest begins, which they believe is good for the voice. The various song forms include solo and dialogue singing. All songs, apart from a few based on classic scores, are improvised.

Such a meeting usually lasts about ten days. Prizes are given on the closing day. During the meeting, there are also such activities as horse racing, snatching-the-sheep contests, girl-chasing-after-boy games, wrestling, tug-of-war and shooting.

Kazak people's Aken Songfest.

15. Jingpo People's *Munaozongge* Gathering

Monaozongge is a festive day for the Jingpo people in Yunnan, taking place usually during harvest time on a chosen day.

Munaozongge is a transliteration of a Jingpo word meaning group singing and dance. An old Jingpo legend says: "Long, long ago, only the children of the Sun God knew how to dance. Once, the Sun God sent messengers to invite all things on earth to a *munaozongge* meeting. The clever lark was chosen to represent the earth and attend. Having learned the art of singing and dancing, the lark, back from the sun, recommended that the peacock act as the *naoshuang* (the leading dancer) and give a performance on earth. Shenglagongzha and his wife, forebears of the Jingpo people, who happened to be around and see this splendid performance, were so enchanted by it that they passed on the *munaozongge* to their own people in the hope that their children and children's children could all enjoy it and live forever in happiness.

At a *munaozongge* in the early morning, people of all nationalities in the mountain area come to the site of dancing to extend greetings to their Jingpo brothers and sisters: the Dais come dancing the peacock dance, the Achang people come beating drums and gongs, the Benlong people come firing muskets and setting off firecrackers and the Lisu people come playing three-stringed instruments. . . .

The whole place is aflame with colours. At the centre of the stage stand four wooden planks (*munaoshidong*), which have drawings of dancers on them. On the bamboo terraces flanking the stage fly coloured pennants. Behind the stage is a *huge* wooden drum with several big gongs hanging on both sides. Two big swords, sacrosanct-looking and awe-inspiring, stand crossways between the *munaoshidong*.

Before the meeting begins, a group of Jingpo men and women, holding in both hands rice wine, sticky-rice cakes and dates, walk into the site to welcome the guests of other nationalities. When the sun is coming up from the horizon, Jingpo men send up rockets into sky to declare the meeting open. In the strains of the high-sounding *dongba* (a kind of musical instrument like an oxhorn) and the pleasant rhythms of the flute, thousands of people enter the site in firm dancing steps, men holding long glistening swords like soldiers going to the front, and the shapely Jingpo girls as pretty as butterflies. The girl chosen as the *naoshuang*, with a headdress ornamented with peacock feathers (symbol of good luck) and a dazzling necklace dangling in front of her chest, wears an eye-catching colourful skirt with floral designs on it. Thousands upon thousands of dancers, in keeping with the beats of the drums and the joyful rhythms, come in one by one, now going forward with heads uplifted, now going around with heads bowing low. When those at the head rock, others in the rear roll; together they move on like a huge dragon wriggling.

This often continues from early morning to evening, or even through the night, lasting for several days.

16. Jing People's Song Festival (Ha Jie)

Ha Jie is a traditional festival of the Jing people living around Dongxing County in Guangxi. *Ha* is a Jing word meaning singing. The date of the festival varies from place to place, falling on the tenth day of the sixth lunar month in some places, on the tenth day of the eighth month in other places, and on the fifteenth day of the first month in still other places.

A story about the Song Festival goes: About seven or eight hundred years ago, a singing fairy came to the place where the Jing people lived. Everyday after work, he enthusiastically taught people singing. His songs, which exposed and lashed at the evil doings of the rulers and gave expression to the people's

Jingpo people's *Munaozongge* Gathering legend.

longing for freedom and happiness, were welcomed by the Jing people. To commemorate him, the Jing people built a "Ha" pavilion where they sang and taught others to sing. This activity was handed down from generation to generation and eventually was developed into the present-day Ha Jie.

The Ha pavilion where the local inhabitants sing at the festival is a wooden well-constructed building, with a fine exterior and a strong national style of its own. The songs for the festival are based on a hand-written songbook and sung by professionals, usually one man and two women who sing in turn. These songs tell the story of a historical figure, narrate a folk tale, describe the happy life, or praise friendship and love. There is always a big audience, including people of both the Han and Zhuang nationalities, sometimes as many as several thousands.

Folk Customs at Other Festivities of the Minority Peoples in China

The Mongolian New Year: The Mongolian New Year falls on the first lunar month, described as "the white month." In ancient times, the Mongolians regarded white colour the mother of everything, the symbol of a pure mind. Marco Polo in his book on his impressions of the East wrote that the Mongolians, including the Great Khan, his ministers and subjects, all wore white clothes according to an ancient custom on the New Year Day, that is, beginning from the first of the first month — all in white garments. During the festival, he observed, people exchanged things in white as gifts, regarding white clothes as the auspicious dress. Marco Polo also described the scene of the Mongols' New Year celebrations in the Yuan Dynasty. On that day, he said, tributes of over a hundred thousand most splendid white horses were sent from some parts of the country to the capital. On that day, there were about five thousand elephants, draped with caparisons each carrying on the back two magnificent boxes filled with gold and silver wares and armours to be used by the imperial household on the White Festival. There were countless numbers of camels, also decorated with caparisons, carrying new things needed for the day. They marched past the Great Khan to present the most spectacular parade in the world.

Today, the Mongolian people wear new clothes during the New Year, exchange greetings and give New Year presents to each other, and offer *hata* to each other. On the New Year Eve elderly people are offered "the wine to bid farewell to the outgoing year." On New Year's Day, people ride horses to visit friends, often to be entertained by the hosts with a whole-sheep feast.

The Daurs' New Year: In the Daur language, the lunar new year is called *anie*. On the thirteenth of the twelfth month, they offer sacrifices to forebears and sweep clean their tombs. Every family cleans its courtyard and piles up a heap of dried cow dung in front of the main entrance. When it burns in the evening, the fires of so many households send up flames sky-high to create an atmosphere of amity and auspiciousness in the village. People sit up late on the New Year Eve. They hang various kinds of lanterns outside the front doors, some being ice lanterns. On New Year's Day, people dress up and wish the elderly people in the family good health, offer them a pipe of tobacco and kowtow to them and extend New Year greetings to neighbours, house by house. Every household has steamed cakes ready for the guests. The moment visitors step into somebody's house, they will hasten to go to the kitchen, remove the lid on the cauldron and scramble to eat the cakes contained there. They will then give their opinions on the cakes they have tasted and compare them with those they had at the other households. If the cake tastes very sweet, the maker of the cake is supposed to be good-natured and kind-hearted. Generally speaking, during a call, visitors and hosts alike, male or female, must exchange cigarettes or a pipe of tobacco as a sign of respect. Girls at the Spring Festival dancing party bring along pouches they have embroidered themselves and quietly give them to their sweethearts as a token of affection. Daurs during the *anie* have many recreational games. Like the Mongolians, they have wrestling, horse racing and archery contests and are particularly fond of playing *bei kuo*, a kind of game similar to ice hockey. Celebrations last until the sixteenth day of the month. The last day of the celebrations is called the "Black Soot Day," on which everybody smears his or her face with soot. It is said that failure to do so will bring bad luck in the year. So, young people all stain their hands with soot to smear other people's faces. Girls become the favourite targets and their faces are often smeared black by young men.

The Yao New Year: The first of the first lunar month is the Yao people's New Year Day. There are gatherings attended by girls wearing jackets and skirts with floral designs, and fine silver ornaments, and by boys also in their holiday best. At the beginning of the gathering, three young people give a performance on farming, one disguised as an ox, the other as a farmer at a plough and the third one as another farmer carrying a hoe. The trio sing and dance in hope of a good harvest in the coming year and a good Spring Festival. People visit each other to exchange greetings and attend shooting and other events.

Yao People's Day of Singing: This is a gathering of the Yao people to celebrate a good harvest. It takes place every year on the sixteenth day of the tenth lunar month. It is also a day when young people meet and court each other through dialogue singing.

Onghor Festival: A festive day on which the Tibetans celebrate in advance a good harvest. Usually it begins on an auspicious day before autumn harvest and lasts one to three days. During the festival, people in their holiday best ride on horses and roam in the fields. They then gather to pitch tents on forest clearings, put coloured cushions on the ground, and spread picnics of sour milk and good food. Some begin to play the six-stringed lute, others sing and dance to celebrate in advance a good harvest. The festival is also the occasion for such sports activities as horse racing and archery. In the race course, picking up *hata* is a very interesting event. Riders, while spurring their horses along a specified course, try and pick up *hata* on the ground. Those who ride faster and pick up more win. The event will go on until dark. Only then do people begin to go home, singing and dancing on the way.

Dama Festival: A traditional festival of the Tibetans. Every year around the fourteenth day of the sixth lunar month they gather for horse racing, ox racing and archery contests on horseback. People of both sexes and of all ages come to attend. The most interesting events are horse racing and sports on horseback. Most riders who vie for the awards are adolescents and teenagers. The festival also has a fair where people trade farm produce and animal products.

Xuedun Festival: One of the traditional Tibetan festivals. *Xue* means sour milk and *dun*, feast. Before the 17th century, *xue dun* was a purely religious activity. Later it gradually developed into a Tibetan theatrical festival. It takes place every year on the thirtieth of the sixth lunar month.

Sagedawa Festival: The festival with which the Tibetan lamaists mark Sakyamuni's birthday, the day he was said to have become the Buddha and also the day of his death. It is also the day the Tibetans, both monastic and lay, celebrate in advance a good harvest. It takes place every year on the fifteenth of the fourth month on the Tibetan calendar. It has been observed for more than a thousand years. It is also said to be the day Princess Wen Cheng of the Tang Dynasty arrived in Tibet and so there are commemorative activities in all parts of Tibet.

April the Eighth Festival: (1) An important festival of the Miaos living in the counties of Guiyang City, Guizhou Province. Beginning from the Ming Dynasty, every year on the eighth day of the fourth lunar month, young people of the Miao nationality, in festival dress, assemble at the fountain in Guiyang City to sing and commemorate their legendary national hero Yanu. Since Liberation, it has become a gathering of people of different nationalities for friendship and solidarity. (2) One of the festivals of the Bouyei people. The name for the festival varies from place to place. In some places, it is called *Niuwang* Jie (Cattle King Day), in other places, the Mutong Jie (Cowherds Day) or Kaiyang Jie (Planting Rice Saplings Day). On that day, both men and cattle eat glutinous rice and have a day off, a treat to the beast of burden.

New Year Festival: The Yi people celebrate their New Year in the tenth lunar month. On the occasion, cattle, sheep and pigs are slaughtered as sacrifices to their ancestors. In the past in Liangshan, the subordinates had to dedicate half of a pig's head to their superiors as a gesture of subordination. The Yis drink wine, sing songs and exchange greetings on that day. In the night, young people gather at clearings in pine tree forests or on an open field to dance the moon dance. Men play the three-stringed instrument, or the lute, accompanied by the flute, and dance with women in pairs. The dance movements include three steps forward and a double-time pause and lifting a foot forward, or spinning on the spot and clapping hands.

Mawlid al-Nabi Festival: It falls on the twelfth day of the third month on the Islamic calendar. It is a day commemorating Mohammed, founder of Islam. He was born in the third month and died in another third month on the Islamic calendar. The basic canon of Islam is: Believe in Allah as the one and only diety in the universe and in Mohammed as Allah's messenger.

March the Third Festival: A traditional festival of the Meifu tribe of the Li people on Hainan Island. Every year on the third day of the third lunar month, they attend an assembly to celebrate in advance a bountiful harvest of *shan lan* (dry rice grown in mountains) and a good hunt. It is also the time for young people to look for sweethearts.

Spring Ox Dance: A unique event taking place among the Dong people on the day of the Beginning of Spring (Li Chun).

The ox-head is made of bamboo covered with paper. The head is decorated with a big red flower and the body is covered with a cotton-quilted blanket with a few token ox-hair on it. Two young men act as the ox and dance, followed by other performers as peasants carrying ploughs and peasant women carrying baskets. The company goes to every household to say: "Spring ox comes to your doorstep and may the weather be good enough to promise a good harvest!" The master of the house serves the company with brown sugar and sticky-rice cakes to show his gratitude.

Eating-New-Rice Day: The Miao people's ancient traditional festivity, every year on the sixth of the sixth lunar month. It is the season when mid rice ripens and a harvest is in sight. Every household will pull up three rice plants in the ear from the field, wash and steam them with rice for the whole family to have a try, known as eating the new rice. It is said that this festival is observed to commemorate a heroic man who worked all his life for public welfare. The Miao people wear their festival dress that day, blow the *lusheng*, sing songs and take part in horse racing and bird fighting.

Dragon Boat Festival: A Miao people's festive day, from the twenty-third to twenty-seventh of the fifth lunar month; in some places, on the fifth of the fifth month. The main event on that day is a dragon boat regatta. Often, tens of thousands of people line the river banks to watch the event.

Kuzhazha Festival: An annual festive day of the Hanis. *Kuzhazha* in Hani means "let there be a good harvest and men and animal enjoy good health." The Hani people have many offshoots, whose time for the festive celebrations varies, generally in midsummer in the sixth lunar month, lasting three to five days.

Flower Dance Meet: A festive day of the Bouyeis which takes place every year between the first of the first lunar month to the twenty-first, usually on a large flat grass field. Participants number from several thousand to over ten thousand. After the meet, people will get ready for spring ploughing.

Lamp Festival: Taer Monastery, a sacred place of Buddhism, is located at Huangzhong County, Qinghai Province. A grand lamp festival takes place here every year on the fifteenth day of the first lunar month. It is attended by people in the locality and those from afar, including the Tibetans, the Mongolians, the Tus, the Hans and the Huis, upwards of tens of thousands. During the festival, the halls in the monastery are decorated with colourful lamps and there is a religious rite in the form of dancing the socerers' dance. The festival usually lasts seven days.

Plucking Flowers Day: A festive day of the people of the Benglong and Dai nationalities observed every year at the Qing Ming Festival. On that day, everybody, men and women, old and young, put on their best holiday dresses and go together to mountains or woods nearby to pluck flowers to give to friends as a kind of blessing. These flowers are also used to decorate their own houses.

Good Harvest Ritual: A festival day of the Gaoshan people in Taiwan Province. It takes place on a chosen day after autumn harvest, lasting three to five days. During the festival, there is a grand gathering for singing and dancing. The most popular dance is the hand-in-hand dance. The number of dancers can be limitless: from three or five to over a dozen, scores or even a few hundred. The singing includes songs dedicated to forebears or national heroes, harvest songs and song for solidarity. Sometimes, the words of the songs are improvised.

APPENDICES

1. The Twenty-four Solar Terms

The twenty-four solar terms are part and parcel of the Chinese farming (lunar) calendar. Our forebears, with long years of experience in farming, gradually came to grasp the laws governing the changes of the four seasons and the climate. They divided the whole year into twenty-four parts under twenty-four solar terms to help mark the seasonal changes, fluctuations of termperature, the dry and rainy seasons and the growing cycles. The result is the sum of the experience of the Chinese toiling masses in matching work to season and is a basic contribution to the development of agricultural production in China.

The system of the twenty-four solar terms did not reach perfection all at once. Early in the Spring and Autumn Period, the *Book of Historical Documents* already referred to the Summer Solstice as *ri yong* (lasting daytime) and to the Winter Solstice as *ri duan* (short daytime). The *Master·Lu's Spring and Autumn Annals* written at the close of the Warring States period mentioned unmistakably the four solar terms: the Beginnings of Spring, Summer, Autumn and Winter. In those days, people erected a rod on the ground and measured the length of its shadow under the sun to determine the solstices. The day of the Winter Solstice is the day the shadow is the longest; the day of Summer Solstice is the day the shadow is the shortest; and the days of the Vernal Equinox and the Autumnal Equinox are the days the length of the shadow of the rod lies between the shortest and the longest. These eight solar terms divide a year precisely into eight periods of time, basically of the same length, thereby fixing the period of time for the four seasons. This was utterly necessary for developing agricultural production. Xun Zi, an ancient Chinese philosopher (*circa* 313-238 B.C.), once spoke of ploughing in spring, weeding in summer, harvesting in autumn and garnering food in winter. By the Qin and Han dynasties, about 2,100 years ago, the division of the year into twenty-four solar terms had been well established. *The Book of the Prince of Huai Nan*, written by Liu An and others in the Western Han Dynasty, listed the twenty-four solar terms exactly in the same way as they are today.

Based on the rotation of the four seasons in cyclic order, the twenty-four solar terms reflect the revolution of the earth around the sun. They belong entirely to that part of the solar calendar adopted by the farming calendar. From the astronomical point of view, these terms are determined by the position of the sun on the ecliptic. The ecliptic is divided into 360 degrees. The two points at which the ecliptic and the equator meet are the point of Vernal Equinox and that of Autumnal Equinox respectively. The former is located at zero degrees, celestial longitude, and the later, at 180 degrees. The whole ecliptic is divided into 24 sections each of which is divided into 15 degrees, and the point where two sections meet is a solar term. Thus, each term falls in the main on a fixed day on the Gregorian calendar, with a difference of no more than a day in different years; on the farming or lunar calendar, however, the dates of these terms are irregular, with a difference possibly of many days in different years.

The twenty-four solar terms were first introduced to peasants in the middle and lower reaches of the Yellow River, and were gradually popularized in other parts of the country. It must be pointed out that these terms are more closely related to the climate and farm work in the middle and lower reaches of the river.

Li Chun, Beginning of Spring. The first solar term in the Chinese farming (lunar) calendar. If and when that day is a fine day, it portends a good harvest for the year.

Yu Shui, Rain Water. The weather gets warm after Yu Shui, generally with no more snowfall. In most parts of China, rainfall gradually increases.

Jing Zhe, Waking of the Insects. By now the weather is rather warm and sometimes there is spring thunder. Animals which have been hibernating will come out of the earth and resume their activities. In most parts of China, it is the season for spring ploughing. A farmers' axiom in central China says: "After the Day of Jing Zhe, spring ploughing continues without letup."

Chun Fen, Vernal Equinox. "Chun Fen means an equal division between *yang* (positive) and *yin* (negative), and so, the night is as long as the day and the weather is neither cold nor hot." (*Luxuriant Dew from the "Spring and Autumn Annals"*, by Dong Zhongshu of the Western Han Dynasty). On this day, the sunlight beams vertically on the equator and the night and the day are almost of the same length. In most parts of China, winter crops begin to grow. A farmers' axiom in central China says: "Wheat stands up to grow on Chun Fen Day, no time is to be wasted for a short while is worth a thousand taels of gold."

Qing Ming, Clear and Bright. The mercury begins to rise, with the mean temperature at the middle and lower reaches of the Yellow River and in areas to its south going up to more than 10°C. In most parts of the country, there is warm weather, trees begin to bud, and wintry scenes are nowhere to be seen.

Gu Yu, Rain for Grain. In ancient times, Gu Yu implied that "all kinds of cereals grow in rain." Around the time of Gu Yu, the weather is usually very warm and there is an increase in rainfall. In north China, it is a busy season during which spring crops are planted and begin to sprout. A farmers' axiom in the north says: "Around the time of Gu Yu, sow melon seeds and seed the fields with beans."

Li Xia, Beginning of Summer. By now people are busy working in the fields and crops are growing fast. A farmers' axiom says: "All fields should be weeded for three days in a row after Li Xia."

Xiao Man, Grain Full. In north China summer crops at this time of the year are full; in the south it is time for summer harvest and summer sowing.

Mang Zhong, Grain in Ear. *Mang* in Chinese means crops with awns, and *zong*, seeds. At this time of the year, both wheat and barley begin to grow awns. In the middle and lower reaches of the Yangtze River, it is the rainy season. In farming, people are still busily engaged in summer harvest and summer sowing.

Xia Zhi, Summer Solstice. On this day, the sun beams almost vertically on the Tropic of Cancer; in the northern hemisphere, the daytime is the longest in a year. By now, the fast-growing crops are being threatened by weeds and pests, which, too, are spreading fast. Field management needs to be intensified. A farmers' axiom in central China says: "On Summer Solstice Day, cotton fields are overgrown with weeds, which are more dangerous than a poisonous snake snapping at someone."

Xiao Shu, Slight Heat. This is about the beginning of the dog days. In most parts of China the weather is the hottest in a year. In farming, people are busily looking after the summer and autumn crops.

Da Shu, Great Heat. This is about the middle of the dog days. In many parts of China, it is the hottest season, also the season in which warm-weather crops grow fastest.

Li Qiu, Beginning of Autumn. After Li Qiu, temperatures begin to drop. In central China, people begin to bring in the early rice and transplant the late rice.

Chu Shu, Limit of Heat. In most parts of China the mercury keeps falling.

Bai Lu, White Dew. In most places in China, the weather gets cooler and temperature drops sharply. At night, vapour in the air which gets chilled is condensed upon trees and flowers to become droplets.

Qiu Fen, Autumnal Equinox. "Qiu Fen means an equal division between *yin* and *yang*, and so, the night is again as long as the day and the weather is neither cold nor hot." (*Luxuriant Dew from the "Spring and Autumn Annals."*) Like the Vernal Equinox, the sunlight beams almost vertically on the Equator and daytime and nighttime are equally long. In north China, autumn harvest and autumn sowing begin.

Han Lu, Cold Dew. By this time, temperature is low and dews become icy cold. In most parts of China, autumn harvest and autumn sowing begin.

Shuang Jiang, Frost's Descent. The weather gets cold. Moisture is condensed on tree leaves and branches or on the ground to form frost. Frost comes to the Yellow River valley sometime around this day. In the south, it is the busy season for autumn harvest and autumn sowing.

Li Dong, Beginning of Winter. By then, water freezes up in the middle and lower reaches of the Yellow River. Construction of water conservancy works starts throughout the country.

Xiao Xue, Slight Snow. Snowing begins in the Yellow River basin.

Da Xue, Heavy Snow. In the Yellow River valley there are snow drifts. A farmers' axiom says: "Snow whirls around the time of Da Xue and Dong Zhi, time for engaging in sideline production and collecting more manure."

Dong Zhi, Winter Solstice. The sunlight beams almost vertically on the Tropic of Capricorn and in the northern hemisphere daytime is the shortest in a year. In most places in China, countryside people take measures against frostbite, start collecting manure and deep ploughing. They also see that the domestic animals pass the winter safely.

Xiao Han, Slight Cold. "In the early twelfth month, it is not yet very cold. But after the middle of the month, the weather

The Twenty-four Solar Terms in Their Proper Order and Their Dates on the Gregorian Calendar

Solar Term	Gregorian Date	Lunar Date	Solar Term	Gregorian Date	Lunar Date
Li Chun	Feb. 4 or 5	early 1st month	Li Qiu	Aug. 7 or 8	early 7th month
Yu Shui	Feb. 19 or 20	mid 1st month	Chu Shu	Aug. 23 or 24	mid 7th month
Jing Zhe	Mar. 5 or 6	early 2nd month	Bai Lu	Sept. 7 or 8	early 8th month
Chun Fen	Mar. 20 or 21	mid 2nd month	Qiu Fen	Sept. 23 or 24	mid 8th month
Qing Ming	Apr. 4 or 5	early 3rd month	Han Lu	Oct. 8 or 9	early 9th month
Gu Yu	Apr. 20 or 21	mid 3rd month	Shuang Jiang	Oct. 23 or 24	mid 9th month
Li Xia	May 5 or 6	early 4th month	Li Dong	Nov. 7 or 8	early 10th month
Xiao Man	May 21 or 22	mid 4th month	Xiao Xue	Nov. 22 or 23	mid 10th month
Mang Zhong	Jun. 5 or 6	early 5th month	Da Xue	Dec. 7 or 8	early 11th month
Xia Zhi	Jun. 21 or 22	mid 5th month	Dong Zhi	Dec. 21 or 22	mid 11th month
Xiao Shu	Jul. 7 or 8	early 6th month	Xiao Han	Jan. 5 or 6	early 12th month
Da Shu	Jul. 23 or 24	mid 6th month	Da Han	Jan. 20 or 21	mid 12th month

gets severely cold." This is about the coldest time in a year. In most parts of China, it is severely cold.

Da Han, Severe Cold. The last of the twenty-four solar terms. By then, in most parts of the country come the coldest days of the year.

2. The Ten Heavenly Stems and Twelve Earthly Branches

In the Chinese farming calendar, years are not counted by numbers but by a method of combining the "stems and branches" (*gan zhi*). This method has been in use in China for more than two thousand years. It is a major invention in the ancient Chinese calendar system.

Gan, or stems, is also known as the *tian gan*, or Heavenly Stems, represented by ten Chinese characters: *jia, yi, bing, ding, wu, ji, geng, xin, ren* and *gui*, and in that order. *Zhi*, or branches, is also known as *di zhi*, or Earthly Branches, represented by twelve Chinese characters: *zi, chou, yin, mao, chen, si, wu, wei, shen, you, xu* and *hai* and in that order.

The counting of years by the Stems and Branches System is to combine each of the ten characters representing the Heavenly Stems with each of the twelve characters representing the Earthly Branches. This makes sixty combinations, known as a *jiazi*, or a *huajia*. According to the combinations in the order of these characters, the first year of a sixty-year cycle (*jiazi*) is the combination of the first character of the Heavenly Stems with the first character of the Earthly Branches, i.e., Jiazi, the second year, *Yichou*, and the third year *Bingyin*.... Thus, historical events in modern Chinese history are denoted in this way. For instance, the Sino-Japanese War of 1894 is the War of *Jiawu*; the Reform Movement of 1898 is known as the

Reform Movement of *Wuxu*; and the Revolution of 1911 is called the *Xinhai* Revolution.

3. The Twelve Animals Denoting Years People Are Born in

Ancient astrologists in China paired off twelve animals with the Twelve Earthly Branches. Thus, *zi* is rat, *chou* is ox, *yin* is tiger, *mao* is rabbit, *chen* is dragon, *si* is snake, *wu* is horse, *wei* is sheep, *shen* is monkey, *you* is cock, *xu* is dog and *hai* is pig. Thus, the year 1984, the year of *Jiazi* in the lunar calendar, is called the year of the rat. The year 1985, the year of *Yichou*, is the year of the ox. A person born in a year of a particular animal is said to be under the sign of that animal. Thus, if one is born in the year of *zi*, one is under the sign of the rat. This is called the Twelve Animals or the Twelve Signs.

4. Modern China's Commemorative Days

January 1   New Year's Day, a one-day national holiday.

March 8   International Working Women's Day (1910), a holiday for women.

May 1   International Labour Day (1889), a one-day national holiday.

May 4   China Youth Day (1919).

June 1   International Children's Day (1949), a one-day holiday for Children.

July 1   Anniversary day of the founding of the Communist Party of China (1921).

August 1   The Chinese People's Liberation Army Day (1927).

October 1 The anniversary day of the founding of the People's Republic of China (1949), a two-day national holiday.

5. A Brief Chinese Chronology

XIA   circa 21st century B.C. — 16th century B.C.
SHANG   circa 16th century B.C. — 11th century B.C.
WESTERN ZHOU   circa 11th century B.C. — 771 B.C.
EASTERN ZHOU
   Spring and Autumn Period   770 B.C. — 476 B.C.
   Warring States Period   475 B.C. — 221 B.C.
QIN   221 B.C. — 207 B.C.
WESTERN HAN   206 B.C. — A.D. 25
EASTERN HAN   25 — 220
THREE KINGDOMS (Wei, Shu, Wu)   220 — 265
WESTERN JIN   265 — 316
EASTERN JIN   317 — 420
SOUTHERN AND NORTHERN DYNASTIES   420 — 589
SUI   581 — 618
TANG   618 — 907
FIVE DYNASTIES AND TEN STATES   907 — 960
NORTHERN AND SOUTHERN SONG   960 — 1279
LIAO   916 — 1125
KIN   1115 — 1234
YUAN   1271 — 1368
MING   1368 — 1644
QING   1644 — 1911

中国传统节日民俗

齐星　编著

杨光华　绘图

＊

外文出版社出版
（中国北京百万庄路24号）
外文印刷厂印刷
中国国际图书贸易总公司
（中国国际书店）发行
北京 399 信箱
1988年（34开）第一版
（英）
I S B N　7 —119—00451 — 4 / K · 26（外）
00395
11 — E —1980P